THE BRITISH EMPIRICISTS

THE
BRITISH
EMPIRICISTS
LOCKE · BERKELEY · HUME

By JAMES COLLINS

PROFESSOR OF PHILOSOPHY
ST. LOUIS UNIVERSITY

THE BRUCE PUBLISHING COMPANY / Milwaukee

Library of Congress Catalog Card Number: 67-26506

PREFACE

MODERN philosophy takes a distinctive turn as a result of the work done in Great Britain during the period 1670–1780. This age opens with Locke's reflections upon the nature of the human understanding. He places the emphasis upon making an operational analysis of the mind at work, upon underlining the limits and degrees of knowledge, and upon making one's report in clear philosophical prose. The commitment of philosophy to the epistemological problem is further strengthened by Berkeley's careful study of the basic components in knowledge, the language we use in daily life as well as in argumentation, and the correlation between our view of the self and of God. With Hume, the modest range of our cognitive power and the restricted nature of its objects are compared with the vaulting aims of the traditional philosophical systems. The consequence is a mitigated skepticism about our knowledge-claims, but one that encourages a constant probing into human nature and its practical tendencies in everyday life.

It would be misleading to conclude, however, that the British empiricists are occupied exclusively with questions about sense data and cognition. There are three circumstances that lead them to broaden their philosophical horizons beyond a narrow epistemological interest. First, they keep their thinking remarkably open to the changes going on in contemporary science. In this respect, each of the classical empiricists establishes a unique relationship with some facet of scientific research. In Locke's case, his early association with Robert Boyle and his own professional training as a physician lead him to respect the distinctive use of the mind in biological and chemical research, which cannot be reduced simply to the mathematico-physical model. Berkeley and Hume, on the other hand, reflect the massive impact of Newton on science and the popular outlook. Berkeley takes an interest in the objectivity of mathematical reasoning and the formalism involved in physical laws. Hume's aim is to become the Newton of the moral world, that is, to extend the general pattern of Newtonian reasoning into the area of humane questions.

A second broadening influence is that exerted by the continental rationalists themselves. There is nothing insular about the British empiricists. All of them are careful readers of the rationalist source works, maintain correspondence with friends of the rationalist persuasion, and share some important traits in common with them. Locke, for instance, refuses to take a reductive, single-level view of the sources of experience. These sources remain irreducibly plural, since reflection makes a contribution distinct in some respect from that of sensation. The mind's active power of attending and reflecting, comparing and inferring, is recognized by all the empiricists, distinguishing their position fundamentally from a flat sensualism. Berkeley's distinction between image and idea, sense datum and active self, brings out the complexity of his analysis of the life of intelligence. And although Hume worries lest such acknowledgments should wipe out all controls over our philosophical statements, nevertheless he bases some of his most important conclusions upon a theory about reason and an explanatory distinction between impressions of sensation and those of reflection.

A third element shared by the empiricists is their steady concern for the exigencies of practical life. There is an explicit moral motif in all their philosophies which effectively prevents any comfortable sealing off of their thought in an epistemological cylinder. They like to wrestle with the question of how a philosophical sort of ethics and a viable social outlook can be developed, even after the defects of metaphysics in the systematic manner have been exposed. Their answer is that the foundations of ethical, political, and religious life rest, not upon general metaphysical premises, but rather upon a careful scrutiny of human nature and the phenomena of human action considered directly in themselves.

To point out these shared features of their thought is not to say that Locke, Berkeley, and Hume are interesting only as members of a trio. Each philosopher remains very much his own man, and lays down his own roadbed of principles of inquiry. But together, they do embody a style of philosophizing which takes a unique approach to man and his problems, and whose further potentialities are still being explored. In this separate publishing of Chapters 8, 9, and 10 of my *History of Modern European Philosophy,* I use the opportunity to make a few corrections in the main text and to continue up-dating the Bibliographical Notes.

JAMES COLLINS

Saint Louis University
June, 1967

CONTENTS

Chapter I. JOHN LOCKE

I. LIFE AND WRITINGS

LOCKE was born in the small town of Wrington, near Bristol, in 1632. Both from his father and from Westminster School in London, he received a strict, Puritan upbringing. He entered Christ Church, Oxford, in 1652, received the bachelor's and master's degrees there, and held the senior studentship at that college until 1684. While at Oxford, his religious sympathies turned toward the Church of England, since it provided a broader basis for national unity. In later life, Locke agreed with the latitudinarian party that belief in Christ should be the only test of religious fellowship. He regarded his undergraduate training in philosophy as unintelligible, although his own speculation always bore traces of this early "Scholastic" formation. During graduate studies, he received his first introduction to Descartes' writings, an experience that gave him a relish for things philosophical and reassured him that clear and rational thinking was just as possible in philosophy as in the empirical sciences. Most of Locke's active years at Oxford, however, were spent in scientific investigations. During Robert Boyle's stay at Oxford (1654–1668), Locke became the great chemist's close associate and aided him in numerous experiments. Locke himself studied medical subjects but never had more than an informal practice.

In 1667, he joined the household of Lord Ashley, later the first Earl of Shaftesbury. Employed at first as a medical aide, Locke's great practical abilities were soon recognized. He then served as advisor and friend to Shaftesbury, who was moving toward the peak of his political career. When Shaftesbury was made Lord Chancellor (1672), Locke was appointed secretary for the Presentation of Benefices, a post that gave him practical acquaintance with ecclesiastical politics. In the following year, he became secretary to the important Council of Trade and Plantations, acquiring further knowledge of economic matters. But the press of work impaired his health, forcing him to retire to France for a long period (1675–1679), in order to regain his strength. Fortunately, this enforced leisure enabled Locke to develop his own philosophical views. In 1671, a group of five or six friends had gathered with him to discuss the problem of the foundations of revealed religion and morality. They were unable to settle the issue because, as Locke remarked to them, they failed to treat the preliminary question of the scope and objects of our understanding. Locke agreed to submit a paper on the nature of the understanding and knowledge, and thus launched out into the inquiry that led eventually to *An Essay concerning Human Understanding.* Two early drafts were completed in 1671; further expansions were made during his years in France; he continued to work on it after his return to England and during his exile in Holland. Finally, the first edition was published in 1690. Locke continued to revise and add to the *Essay,* in the four editions appearing during his lifetime.

Locke's return from France to England (1679) was not for long. His patron, Shaftesbury, headed the Protestant opposition to James II and was forced to flee to Holland, where he died in 1683. That same year, Locke also exiled himself to Holland, where he kept his movements secret for a while, since his name appeared on the list of eighty-five Englishmen wanted by the government, in connection with Monmouth's unsuccessful rebellion. His health improved in Holland, where he enjoyed the company of the Protestant theologian, Philip van Limborch, and of Jean Le Clerc, who edited the literary journal *Bibliothèque Universelle.* In this journal (1688), Locke published an abstract of his *Essay.* The same year marked the "Glorious Revolution," which drove out James II and installed William and Mary on the British throne, under Whig sponsorship. Locke came back to England early in 1689. He published immediately his controversial *Letter concerning Toleration* (1689), which was followed by two other letters on the same subject (1690 and 1693) and a fragment of a fourth letter. In 1690 appeared not only *An Essay concerning Human Understanding* but also the *Two Treatises of Government,* in which Locke opposed the divine-right theory of sovereignty and offered a defense of the Whig settlement. He also published *Some Thoughts concerning Education* (1693) and *The Reasonableness of Christianity* (1695), books that reflected his lifelong interest in educational and religious matters. This latter preoccupation involved him in a controversy with Bishop Stillingfleet, who traced the Unitarian tendencies of the day to the Lockean "way of ideas." Although broken in health, Locke continued his career of public service, as a member of the new Board of Trade and Plantations (1696–1700). But from 1691 onward, he spent most of his leisure time at Oates, the estate of his friends, the Mashams. Lady Masham was the daughter of the Cambridge Platonist, Ralph Cudworth, and was herself a woman of intelligence and sympathy. Locke retired permanently from public service in 1700, received Newton and other friends at Oates, and died peacefully (1704), while Lady Masham was reading the Psalms to him.

2. THE STANDPOINT OF THE "ESSAY"

With disarming frankness, Locke admits that his "discontinued way of writing" *An Essay concerning Human Understanding* leads to certain defects.[1] His treatment lacks the order, coherence, and structural tightness of a work conceived and executed according to a more systematic plan. His use of common language and customary turns of thought makes an appeal to the reader and yet exposes the argument to the vagueness and ambiguity that surround ordinary usage. The *common-sense* tone of the discussion often enables Locke to take advantage of realistic convictions about the mind and the world that do not follow rigorously from his own principles. Nevertheless, the book also has the strength of its weaknesses: it triumphs over all its defects and becomes the landmark of the movement known as British empiricism. The other leaders in this tradition return to Locke's *Essay,* as the common point of departure for their own speculations. For it is successful in formulating the problems and the method that are characteristic of the *empiricist approach* in philosophy.

Instead of discoursing, at once, about sublime issues concerning the inner nature of God, the fine points of moral doctrine and the precise content of revelation, Locke proposes first to inquire into the nature of the knowing faculty which must be used in such investigations. To bypass the problem of the nature of the understanding is to begin at the wrong end of philosophical inquiry. Locke is a

---

[1] *An Essay concerning Human Understanding,* The Epistle to the Reader (Fraser edition, I, 10). For a succinct and informative introduction to Locke, read R. I. Aaron, "Great Thinkers: (X) John Locke," *Philosophy,* 12 (1937), 19–32; the series of essays on "Great Thinkers" in *Philosophy* is worth examining, since it includes authoritative essays on most of the great modern philosophers.

strong advocate of the *primacy of theory of knowledge* over the metaphysical, ethical, and cosmological branches of philosophy. For, unless the structure and scope of the mind are determined with some precision at the outset, it becomes impossible to eliminate sterile controversies and confine our study to questions where there is some solid hope of gaining certainty, or at least high probability. The modern Ockham's razor is found in this concern to relieve the mind of fruitless issues and direct it only toward matters where it has some competence.

The *purpose* of the *Essay* is stated concisely in the Introduction: "To inquire into the original, certainty, and extent of *human knowledge,* together with the grounds and degrees of *belief, opinion* and *assent.*"[2] This program is reflected in the organization of Locke's materials. In Book I, a negative answer is given to the problem of the origin of knowledge, by showing that innatism is an inadequate explanation. Book II discusses the positive origin of knowledge by means of an analysis of the different kinds of ideas, their relation to experience, and their combination according to the various intellectual operations. A long detour is made in the third book, for the purpose of examining the nature and use of words, with special reference to general terms as signs of essences. Finally, the fourth book applies the previous findings to the main issue: the nature and scope of human knowledge, together with the distinction between knowledge, probability, and belief.

In order to carry out this ambitious project, Locke makes two crucial decisions in the methodological order. The first is to employ only the "historical, plain method"; the second is to take ideas as the primary objects of analysis. (1) The *historical, plain method* is a thoroughly empirical approach to the understanding, considering it precisely in its actual operations and treating its objects precisely as they appear in actual consciousness.[3] When a man observes the conscious workings of the cognitive process, as it goes on within himself, he is following the dictates of this method. Its aim is to copy nature and provide an exact description of the functions of the mind-as-engaged-in-thinking, somewhat as Boyle, Sydenkam, and Newton made a descriptive study of the actual movements of observed bodies. Just as one cannot see the physical world through another man's pair of eyes, so one cannot know the nature of

---

[2] *An Essay concerning Human Understanding,* Introduction, 2 (Fraser, I, 26).
[3] *Ibid.* (Fraser, I, 27).

the understanding merely by examining the written reports of others. As the American radical empiricist, William James, was later to say, one must catch experience on the wing, like a bird in its flight. This requires an introspective attention to our own internal acts.

Metaphysical and physicophysiological considerations are not supposed to come within the purview of the historical, plain method, but Locke finds it hard to respect this restriction. This is evident, for instance, in his reply to Stillingfleet, who had cast suspicion upon Locke's reasonings, because of their novelty and their failure to consult the systematic accounts of other thinkers. In defense of his procedure, Locke calls it *a new history of an old thing,* an explanation of the *common* functions of understanding which nevertheless rests upon one's *own* testimony. Personal exploration of one's own consciousness is needed, both because of the privacy of individual consciousness and the differences among individual minds. This would seem, however, to threaten the validity of generalizations made from findings about one's own cognitive history. Hence Locke adds that the intellectual power and operations are *alike* in most men, that most men are of his own mental size and structure. This is a metaphysical belief, resting upon an appeal to common-sense convictions. Locke also desires to be excused from giving any physiological description of perception and from making metaphysical pronouncements about the essence of mind and the dependence of ideas upon a material basis. But in practice, he must assume that really existing, material things emit imperceptible particles or corpuscles, which strike the organs and brain, agitate the animal spirits or nerves, and thereby produce ideas in the mind. Similarly, he makes at least negative pronouncements about the essence of mind, and probable statements about the relation of cognition to the body. These concessions indicate how difficult it is to elaborate a pure theory of knowledge, apart from commitments about the real world, which gives our cognitions their first impulse and content.

(2) The second major feature of Locke's methodology is to begin with an analysis of the *idea,* defined as "whatsoever is the *object* of the understanding when a man thinks . . . whatever is meant by *phantasm, notion, species,* or *whatever it is which the mind can be employed about in thinking.*"[4] In starting with ideas as the atomic

---

[4] *An Essay concerning Human Understanding,* Introduction, 8 (Fraser, I, 32). J. Buchler, "Act and Object in Locke," *The Philosophical Review,* 46 (1937), 528–535, notes that there is a fundamental ambiguity running through Locke's thought, as to

elements of knowledge, Locke accepts the analytic approach of Descartes and most scientifically inclined thinkers. The two main assumptions of *elementarism* are: (*a*) that the elements into which knowledge can be analytically resolved, are more authentic and reliable starting points than the complex wholes themselves, and (*b*) that the elements remain basically unchanged, whether taken in isolation or in composition. The elementarist viewpoint underplays the uniqueness of complex, cognitive wholes, and overlooks the profound modifications undergone by analytic units, upon their reintegration in the total context. But this method gives Locke assurance that he can determine the limits of knowledge "from the right end," i.e., from a prior examination of the knowing power and its mental building blocks, the ideas. Whereas Bacon and Spinoza advise us to test our abilities by first trying them on definite realities, Locke seeks to ascertain *beforehand* which of the imputed realities fall within the mind's range. By resolving judgments into ideas, in order to gain a starting point, he proposes a way to settle in principle the capacity of human intelligence. From this angle, the aim of empiricism is a highly ambitious and rationalistic one.

The Cartesian influence is prominent in Locke's definition of an idea. Both philosophers agree in making "idea" a capacious enough term to cover the mental objects of sensation and imagination, as well as intellection. They also regard the idea as the direct and proper object of the understanding: what is known directly is the idea itself. Locke adds that the idea should also be treated as a sign or representation of existent things. But it remains that sort of sign which is known first of all in and as itself (instrumental sign), before it conveys information about an independent world. The method of starting with ideas, rather than judgments, encourages the treatment of the idea *primarily as an object,* and only *later on as a sign* representing something else. Locke himself was not unaware of the vexatious problems attaching to the representationist hypothesis. He asked Malebranche how one could ever know whether the idea or picture in the mind is like what it is supposed to represent, when the understanding is barred, by definition, from making any independent acquaintance with the thing, in order to make the com-

---

whether "idea" means an object-of-mind distinct from the act of perceiving or an object-of-mind identical with the perceiving act itself. This may be compared with the dual meaning of "experience" mentioned below, Section 4.

parison.[5] He found this question easier to propound than to answer, unless he were to make a metaphysical surmise about the relation of similarity between the extramental thing, as a cause, and the idea, as its effect in the mind. From a strictly epistemological standpoint, however, he could not make any statements about a "background" class of independent things and hence could not directly test the reliability of ideas as signs. Considerations of this sort had forced Leibniz to transfer the whole question to a nonempirical, metaphysical terrain of essential laws.

For Locke himself, two circumstances tended to soften the impact of his radical limitation of method. For one thing, he viewed his function as that of a humble underlaborer rather than a Cartesian master builder. He expressed the empiricist suspicion of constructing elaborate systems through the pure understanding. His work was to clear out the rubble of overgrown prejudice, so that the philosophical edifice might be erected upon firm, well-prepared ground in experience. Philosophy is nothing but the true knowledge of things. Since "things" include natural entities, human actions, and the signs of natural entities and human actions, Locke accepted the Platonic-Stoic, threefold *division of philosophy* into: physics or natural philosophy, ethics or practical philosophy, and semiotic or logic.[6] Since his own *Essay* deals with ideas and words as signs, Locke assigned it to logic or semiotic, which provides the foundation for any knowledge in the other two fields. Hence he often remarked that his inquiries bore upon our ideas of beings rather than upon beings. The main problem, however, was to provide guidance for *making the passage* from a logic, or theory of knowledge and signs, to a study of the actual physical and moral worlds. Berkeley and Hume concentrated upon the weaknesses in Locke's account of this transition, thus encouraging a detachment of his epistemological views from the rest of his philosophical outlook.

The second qualification placed upon his investigations in the *Essay* contains at the same time Locke's protest against such separate consideration of his theory of knowledge. For the *Essay* has a *practical orientation,* in keeping with the circumstances leading to its com-

---

[5] *An Examination of P. Malebranche's Opinion of Seeing All Things in God,* 52 (*The Philosophical Works of John Locke,* edited by J. A. St. John, II, 454). Locke maintained that his own analysis of ideas for purposes of knowledge was at least more defensible than Malebranche's, since Locke held the empirical origin of ideas in things, rather than in God (as Malebranche taught).

[6] *An Essay concerning Human Understanding,* IV, xxi, 2–4 (Fraser, II, 461–462).

position. If the analysis often leads to the replacement of a claim to certitude by one to probability, Locke is not perturbed by the outcome. For, men must learn to be content with but a narrow sphere of certitude and, for the rest, agree to hold their views as matters of probability and belief. Echoing the words of the Cambridge Platonists about reason as the candle of the Lord, Locke affirms that "the candle that is set up in us shines bright enough for all our purposes."[7] These purposes are mainly practical ones, aiming at the technical and moral ordering of the present life and the preparation for life eternal. *Probability* is a sufficient guide for attaining these ends, provided that it builds around the hard core of a few demonstrative truths. Having renounced the Cartesian pretense to universal demonstrative knowledge as the philosophical ideal, Locke begins the process of opening up more and more room for probability and secular faith as regulative principles of practical intelligence. That this was also a tendency of the Cartesian tradition itself, can be seen from Descartes' defense of valid conjecture and Leibniz' accommodation of the technique of mathematical probabilities to problems in ethics, political and legal philosophy, and history.

3. THE DISCREDITING OF INNATISM

To clear the path for his main thesis on the experiential origin of all knowledge, Locke must first contend with the counterthesis that at least some of our knowledge is due to innate ideas and principles. He takes in a wide arc of opponents: the school philosophy taught at Oxford and in Holland, the speculative doctrine of Descartes, the dogmatism of the Cambridge Platonists, and the moral innatism advanced by Herbert of Cherbury. These thinkers present by no means a united front of common doctrine, so that Locke's criticism is broadly phrased and does not always tell against the particular arguments employed by one or another innatist. Although his reasoning seems flat and obtuse to us today, its historical importance is considerable. The theory of innate knowledge never recovered its full strength, after his vigorous blows were delivered. It is noteworthy that, in his formal discussion of innatism, Locke directs his attack primarily against innate first *principles,* which may be either speculative or practical. But the remainder of his philosophy may be regarded as an indirect but

---

[7] *Ibid.,* Introduction, 5 (Fraser, I, 30).

sustained criticism of the innatist hypothesis. For, in tracing out the actual origin of *ideas* in experience, he implies that, if these components have a purely empirical origin, the principles composed out of ideas must share a similar origin.

Among *speculative principles,* Locke singles out the principles of identity and contradiction as test cases.[8] He does not deny their truth but only the necessity of explaining our knowledge of them by recourse to innatism. Their widespread acceptance can be adequately accounted for on the ground of our having an intuitive grasp of their import. Once the significance of the terms of the propositions is explained, the truth of these propositions is perceived immediately by the normal, mature mind. Assent is given to them because of their *self-evidence,* rendering any appeal to innate equipment otiose. Taking the offensive, Locke declares that the innatist theory suffers from an impenetrable obscurity concerning how such principles can be in the mind in any innate way. For a truth can be "in the mind" only *through actual perception* or *memory.* An innate idea or principle which is said to be present only virtually in the mind, has never been actually perceived and hence has never been there, in any understandable way. If it is present there by the memory, then it can be revived without the aid of outside impressions and, in being recalled, is remembered or perceived as being not entirely new. But our experience shows no case in which a first principle is rendered originally present to the mind through its innate resources, apart from any previous perception or the aid of sense experience.

This argument, based on the meaning of "being in the mind," was the provocation for Leibniz' distinction between the innate truth itself and our thinking or perceiving it. Leibniz declared that universal assent is not advanced as a basis of proof but only as a convincing suasion about the innate origin of first principles. He added that Locke failed to distinguish sufficiently between necessary truths of reason and contingent truths of fact. In the case of the latter propositions, Leibniz was willing to allow the need for sense experience: not, however, to supply the ideas and connections that

---

[8] *Ibid.,* I, i, 4–28; IV, vii, 12–30 (Fraser, I, 39–63; II, 285–291). That the dogmatic use of innate ideas by the Cambridge Platonists was the main target of Locke's attack, was brought out by S. P. Lamprecht, "Locke's Attack upon Innate Ideas," *The Philosophical Review,* 36 (1927), 145–165.

constitute the truth itself, but only to arouse the mind to a definite perceiving of these ideas in the required connections. It is obvious that our *act* of perceiving or thinking about any truth cannot be present in the mind otherwise than by an actual perception or remembrance. But this does not settle the origin of the *active tendency* of the mind to grasp the *meaning-content* of the ideas, which content is distinct from the conscious acts of perceiving or remembering. The content of the principles may be present virtually in the mind, without requiring such conscious acts, somewhat in the way in which the mind contains the suppressed steps in an enthymeme. Locke granted that truths are implicitly present, in the sense that the understanding itself belongs to human nature from the outset, but Leibniz added that the understanding is present precisely as a dynamic aptitude for drawing its principles from its own active dispositions. In the case of truly first principles or truths of reason, moreover, he contended that sense experience was not needed even for the act of thinking about the truths. For his proof, however, Leibniz had to summon the aid of his entire metaphysics. Keeping to the safe but narrow rule of his historical, plain method, Locke would outlaw any complicated metaphysical demonstration and hence would conclude that innatism has no empirical evidence in its favor.

In his zeal to secure the experiential origin of the principles of identity and contradiction, however, Locke went to the opposite extreme from innatism, by calling into question their *universal acceptance* and *scientific value*. He doubted their presence in the minds of children, the illiterate, savages, and idiots; he also added that they serve no useful purpose in scientific investigations. To this extent, they are trifling and not fundamental for all knowledge. One need not become a defender of innatism in order to question this line of criticism. Locke employs three main criteria: that first principles are only present in the mind when they are formally and explicitly stated, in textbook fashion; that they are useless, unless they can serve as the proximate premises for scientific deductions or hypotheses; that they are not genuine principles, unless they may be applied without any guidance from experience. The first rule is a somewhat satirical corrective for the extravagant claims being made by the Cambridge Platonists about the universal presence of first principles, and it is questionable how seriously it is meant by Locke. All that one may conclude from interrogating a child about the principle of contradiction, for instance, is that his apprehension of it is concrete and bound up with particular instances of distinguishing between mustard and sugar, his mother and a stranger. The second criterion is much more significant, since it reveals a conflict between the Cartesian conception of the role of first principles and their actual function in a realistic philosophy and natural science. Descartes assigned a *deductive* function for his first principles, whereas the principle of contradiction serves a *resolutive* function in Thomistic realism and in Newtonian natural science. The dependence of specific propositions upon this principle is by way of a resolution, rather than a deductive derivation. Moreover, the physicist as such need not always complete the reduction of a proposition to the point of establishing its direct relationship with the principle of contradiction. Locke decides nothing about the fruitfulness of this principle, by showing that it does not bear fruit in the way specified by Descartes for first principles. Finally, Locke's remarks about the role of experience are pertinent only for an innatist conception of first principles. In a realistic outlook, our experience of the existent world is required for both the genesis and the application of principles.

Locke deals with *practical first principles* in a somewhat different way. He shows that, although they are no less true than speculative ones, they rest upon some reasoning process, which disqualifies them from being innate. Whether it be the Golden Rule or the precept of keeping contracts or any other moral rule, the proposition is not self-evident and requires a certain amount of inference, in order to be seen as true. Locke does not examine the very widest principle in the moral order — that good should be done and evil avoided — but confines himself to the Golden Rule and other less general precepts. His aim is not to relativize morality but only to show that it supposes the right use of our reasoning power, rather than draws upon an innate reservoir. He suggests that education, custom, and pragmatic needs often lead us to regard as naturally given a moral principle which has, in point of fact, been communicated in a social way and with the aid of implicit reasoning.

Finally, he brings the case down to *innate ideas* as such, by considering those of identity and God. This choice is a shrewd one, since Locke regards the idea of identity as necessary for first speculative principles, and the idea of God as essential for first moral principles (duty implying law, and law a lawgiver). But his arguments are hurried and inconclusive. He attacks the innateness of the idea of identity, by urging his special difficulties about personal identity. How can we be sure that there might not be some sort of sameness between "Socrates and the present mayor of Queenborough,"[9] such that the latter would be the reincarnated soul or consciousness of the former? In regard to the idea of God, Locke recites travelers' reports (which so fascinated the seventeenth century) about conflicting notions of God and even alleged cases where no such notion could be found. But this evidence was insufficient, by itself, to unseat Descartes, however effective it may have been against the English Platonists. Descartes had already forestalled the objection based on differing views of God or even on the absence or denial of the idea of God, by observing that the effect of sense and prejudice is profound enough to distort the idea of God and even to hide the reasons for admitting His existence. Innate ideas can be warped and covered over, without destroying their claim to be innate. It is this latter statement by. Descartes which Locke should have subjected to closer analysis.

Locke goes as far as he can, consonant with his empiricism, in meeting the claims of innatism. He grants that human nature has certain inborn powers, not given by experience. He even admits that the *appetitive* powers are endowed with some innate principles of tendency or action, which incline us toward desire, from the outset of life. But he remains firm in his rejection of any innate *cognitive* principles. The understanding may, indeed, acquire prenatally certain particular sense ideas of hunger, warmth, and pain, based upon the conditions of uterine life. But these ideas are drawn from sense experience and are neither determinate nor universal enough to give rise, of themselves, to first principles. The real purpose of the Lockean polemic against innatism comes out in the remark that we ought not to invoke *special innate sanctions* for our principles of philosophy but should gather our knowledge of universal truths from "the being of things themselves, when duly considered."[10] The doctrine of innate ideas and principles was being used, popularly, to cover all sorts of dogmatic assertions, which one could deny only at the cost of also

---

[9] Locke uses this amusing comparison later on in the *Essay*, II, xxvii, 19 (Fraser, I, 460); cf. I, iii, 3–18 (Fraser, I, 93–107). On the innateness of the idea of God, consult the *Second Set of Objections*, sent to Descartes by Mersenne, who cites missionary tales about the absence of the idea of God among the Huron Indians (*The Philosophical Works of Descartes*, translated by Haldane and Ross, II, 26); Descartes' answer is given in advance, in *The Meditations concerning First Philosophy*, V (Lafleur translation, 61).

[10] *An Essay concerning Human Understanding*, I, iii, 25 (Fraser, I, 117).

denying truths said to be implanted in our minds by God or nature. Locke wants to eliminate this nonempirical way of settling issues. Therefore he suggests that we make a patient study of our ideas, which are undoubted objects of our understanding, and thus discover what means we do have for reaching a well-founded conclusion.

4. THE ANATOMY OF IDEAS

If there are no innate ideas or principles, they must all be drawn from a single source: *experience*. This is Locke's basic positive thesis. But (to employ John Dewey's phrase) "experience" is one of those weasel-words which are capable of many twistings and turnings. Locke takes "experience" sometimes to mean the *operations of experiencing* and sometimes the *objects experienced*. He is using it in the former sense, when he states that the two sources of experience are *sensation* and *reflection*.[11] They are the operations of experiencing, whereby all knowledge is gained. The objects immediately experienced are ideas and, on the basis of the origin of ideas, there is a distinction drawn between sensation and reflection. Sensation receives ideas from the external world of sensible things, whereas reflection draws its materials from the internal operations of the mind. These operations of experience are the twin inlets or sluices, through which all the components of knowledge flow into the mind.

Locke accords a definite *priority* to sensation. It supplies the mind with its unconditionally first ideas, and apart from this source there could be no mental life. In its natal condition, the mind is comparable to an empty cabinet, a blank paper, or a dark room. The ideas of sensation provide, as it were, the mind's initial furniture, its primary stampings, its first dawn of light. Thereafter, the understanding can perform distinctive operations of its own, the observation of which issues in the ideas of reflection. Our own thinking and desiring, action and passion, provide a distinctive fund of ideas which enrich and extend our experience. Human knowledge has a purely *empirical* origin, in that it is constructed with the aid of the operations of sensation and reflection, which provide the mind with the ideas of sensation and reflection.

---

[11] *Ibid.*, II, i, 2–5 (Fraser, II, 121–125). J. W. Yolton, "The Concept of Experience in Locke and Hume," *Journal of the History of Philosophy*, 1 (1963), 53–71, distinguishes in British empiricism between an inductive-descriptive meaning of experience and an epistemic-explanatory meaning. The latter approach requires the distinctive help of reason to furnish explanatory concepts (Locke) and principles (Hume), just as much as does the rationalist view of experience.

Locke's Treatment of Ideas

1. Ideas of sensation and reflection from experience (not from innate source).
2. Simple and complex ideas.
3. Kinds of simple ideas.
   a) From one sense only.
   b) From several senses.
   c) From reflection only.
   d) From sensation and reflection.
4. Kinds of complex ideas (formed by combining, comparing, separating).
   a) Modes (simple and mixed).
   b) Substances (single and collective).
   c) Relations (e.g., cause and effect, identity and diversity, moral rules).
5. Primary, secondary, and tertiary qualities.
6. Abstraction of general ideas.
7. Ideas as determinants of the nature, degrees, extent, and reality of knowledge.

The filiation of our ideas with the dual source in experience is more direct and apparent in some cases than in others. Hence there is a fundamental division of ideas into *simple* and *complex* ones.[12] The distinction is made partly in terms of objective content and partly in terms of cognitive operations. From the standpoint of *content*, a simple idea is defined as a single, unmixed appearance, whereas a complex one involves the compounding of several simple ideas, whether of the same kind or of different kinds. From the *operational* standpoint, there is a striking difference in the mind's role, in each case. It is relatively passive in the reception of simple ideas, whereas it is predominantly active in the forming of complex ideas. Despite these clear-cut distinctions, adjustments are necessary in the treatment of particular cases.

Locke fluctuates between calling the understanding "merely passive" and "for the most part, only passive" in respect to simple ideas.[13] He stresses the *passivity* of the mind, when he wishes to demonstrate the noninnate origin of simple ideas and the objective reliability of their content. But in order to avoid the Hobbesian, mechanistic view of the understanding, he seeks to retain the distinctive nature of *cognitive activity*, even in the first reception of simple ideas of

---

[12] *Ibid.*, II, ii, 1–2 (Fraser, 144–146). See W. C. Swabey, "Locke's Theory of Ideas," *The Philosophical Review*, 42 (1933), 573–593.

[13] Cf. *An Essay concerning Human Understanding*, II, i, 25; ix, 1 (Fraser, I, 142, 183). On the ambiguity in this theory of perception, see W. J. Ellos, "Lockean Perception," *The New Scholasticism*, 39 (1965), 323–329.

sense and reflection. The mind is passive, insofar as it must be initially receptive of simple ideas from the sensible world or its own internal domain. These ideas cannot be invented, and without them the mind would be totally ignorant of what transpires within itself and in the outer world. Simple ideas seem to force an entrance and can neither be blotted out nor altered in their main lines. Still, cognitive experience is an activity of man, even though it requires a receptive aspect. Perception, the basic act of the understanding, cannot occur without at least a *minimal conscious attention,* on the part of the knower. The contents of sense and reflection cannot be "given" to the understanding in experience, without some observation, conscious attending, or taking notice of the data. Locke comes much closer to Descartes than to Hobbes in his notion of experience, to the extent that he stresses the factor of mental attention over that of a mere mechanistic reaction to external stimuli, even at the outset of perception.

Sensation and reflection provide a principle of division among simple ideas. Simple ideas belong to four classes, depending upon whether they are received through: one sense only, several senses, reflection only, or both sense and reflection.[14] (*a*) In the first class are included ideas of particular sounds, colors, tastes, smells, and tangible traits (especially solidity). There is a special adaptation of the *individual sense power* to the reception of ideas from the corresponding aspect of the thing. (*b*) Through the co-operation of *several senses* — notably, sight and touch — the mind acquires the following ideas: extension, figure, rest, and motion. (*c*) From *reflection* upon its own operations, the mind acquires a special group of ideas, all of which can be classified as ideas of perception or ideas of volition. Under perception or thinking are included ideas of the acts of discerning, remembering, judging, knowing, believing, etc. The different passions and modes of willing give rise to ideas of volition. (*d*) The final division consists of the ideas of pleasure and pain, existence and unity, power and succession, all of which are derived from both *sense* and *reflection*. All other ideas result from various combinations of these primary ones, and all knowledge is framed with their help.

The active power of the mind comes much more to the fore in the formation of new complex ideas, out of the original stock of simple ones. Among the relevant acts of the mind, Locke emphasizes: *combining, comparing,* and *separating.* It is difficult to keep an air-

---

[14] *An Essay concerning Human Understanding,* II, iii, 1 (Fraser, I, 148).

tight distinction between these fundamental operations. All complex ideas result from a certain combining and comparing, and at least all general complex ideas also involve some separating or abstraction. However, there is a distinction between combining ideas in such a way as to form a compound unit, and comparing ideas so that they may be viewed together in their relations, without resulting in a compound unit. Separation of a certain trait is, again, a distinct sort of operation, resulting in the formation of abstract, general ideas.

With the aid of these three cognitive operations, Locke tackles the huge task of classifying all our complex ideas. He suggests that they come under three headings: *modes, substances,* and *relations.* Just as the operations cannot be kept entirely separate, so there is a good deal of overlapping in this division of ideas, despite Locke's best efforts. The distinctive character of ideas of substances is particularly difficult to maintain; moreover, the boundary between certain ideas of relation and simple modes, like power, is often crossed. Locke's initial definitions provide the basis for his own more detailed examinations, as well as for the investigations made by subsequent empiricists.

> *Modes* I call such complex ideas which, however compounded, contain not in them the supposition of subsisting by themselves, but are considered as dependences on, or affections of substances. . . . The ideas of *substances* are such combinations of simple ideas as are taken to represent distinct *particular* things subsisting by themselves; in which the supposed or confused idea of substance, such as it is, is always the first and chief. . . . The last sort of complex ideas is that which we call *relation,* which consists in the consideration and comparing one idea with another.[15]

Two common features of these definitions are worth pointing out, at once. First, in keeping with the standpoint of the *Essay,* they are concerned with objects precisely as ideas. They state the definitions of *our ideas* of modes, substances, and relations, rather than the realities as they exist apart from the mind. Second, the definitions high-light the *active role of the mind* in the formation of complex ideas, which result from a "consideration" or a "taking" by the understanding. The reader is thereby prepared to expect a thorough revision of accepted opinions concerning the realistic import of these ideas.

Each of the major kinds of complex ideas contains, in turn, a number of subdivisions. Modes are either *simple* or *mixed,* depending

---

[15] *Ibid.,* II, xii, 4, 6, 7 (Fraser, I, 215–216).

upon whether the mind combines several simple ideas of the same kind or unites together several different kinds of simple ideas. Space, duration, number, and infinity are examples of simple modes; theft, wrestling, hypocrisy, and beauty illustrate the mixed modes. In making simple modes, the mind either follows combinations already existing in nature or else joins the ideas together according to its own intent. Mixed modes, however, are usually put together without any reference to actually existing combinations in nature, and hence are sometimes given the special name _notions,_ to signify that they are the outcome of the mind's own synthesizing operation. Locke does admit that, at least in the first instance, the mind may use _observed complex unities_ as a pattern for its complex modal ideas. Hypocritical actions and a wrestling game may have guided the first formation of the ideas of hypocrisy and wrestling. But Locke insists that, thereafter, men usually derive such ideas at secondhand: from custom, education, and dictionary explanations. In his later treatment of mixed modes, Locke unfortunately depreciates the original derivation from observation and emphasizes almost exclusively the roles of inventiveness, education, and linguistic convention. This leads him to state that these ideas have _no_ other reality and reference than a purely mental one and that, therefore, their truth does not depend upon _any_ correspondence with natural existents. This is an extreme conclusion, since it suppresses his own initial recognition that at least some mixed modes are originally constituted with the aid of observation and practical testing. There is no good reason for denying that the tests of observation and use may also serve as ultimate criteria, even for people who were originally given the mixed modes in a purely conventional way.

Ideas of substances are also of two sorts: single and collective. _Single_ substances, like a man or a sheep, are such as are conceived to exist separately. _Collective_ substances also constitute a single complex idea, by uniting the ideas of several individual substances into that of a single entity: an army of men or a flock of sheep. For purposes of later criticism, Locke draws a sharp contrast between these particular ideas of substances, single and collective, and the general idea of substance as such. He lists several varieties of relations or references of comparison among the various kinds of ideas. The main ones studied in the _Essay_ are: cause and effect, identity and diversity, and the moral relations. This choice of examples is a deliberate one, since it enables Locke to bring his analysis to bear upon the crucial problems of causal relation, personal identity, and moral inference.

5. PROBLEMS CONCERNING IDEAS

Locke is at his best in the analysis of particular ideas. He sets a pattern for the empirical way of approaching a problem, even though his own solutions have not been adopted always by his successors. A selection is made here of his treatment of four major questions: the distinction between primary and secondary qualities, the ideas of substances, the relation of cause and effect, and the nature of the self. The distinctive views of Berkeley and Hume on these four issues cannot be appreciated, without some previous understanding of how they were originally formulated in Locke's mind.

1. *Primary and Secondary Qualities.* Locke admits that almost insuperable difficulties attend his attempt to discuss qualities, in a precise but informal way, within his own epistemological framework. His common-sense approach alternates disconcertingly between references to "qualities" and to "ideas of qualities." Often, what he says about qualities can only be said about mental objects or ideas; conversely, he speaks occasionally about the ideas of qualities as though they were present in extramental things. These difficulties stem, in part, from Locke's loose handling of the problem of secondary qualities. But another source is the conflict, in his mind, between his definition of idea as the direct object of the understanding and the common-sense conviction that what we know directly are real things, and that sense percepts are primarily instruments for achieving such knowledge and only secondarily formal objects of knowledge in their own right.

A *quality* is a power in a real thing to produce ideas of qualities in the mind.[16] Qualities are either primary, secondary, or tertiary. A *primary quality* is a power inseparable from a body, under whatsoever conditions it may be placed and observed by us. It is such a quality as is observed to produce a simple idea in us, an idea that not only corresponds with the real quality but also resembles it. In the full sense, a primary quality is really present in a body and supplies a likeness of itself to the mind. Whether or not the mind

---

[16] *Ibid.*, II, viii, 8–26 (Fraser, I, 169–182). For a clarifying discussion of this somewhat obscure portion of Locke's philosophy, cf. R. Jackson, "Locke's Distinction between Primary and Secondary Qualities," *Mind*, N. S., 38 (1929), 56–76.

actually perceives the quality, it is really present in the thing. As for a *secondary quality,* it is nothing real in the thing, except a "bare power" to produce an idea in the percipient subject. This power can operate only by means of the primary qualities of insensible parts of bodies, and is sometimes described by Locke as being nothing more than a certain combination, proportion, or texture found among the primary powers. Although there is a *conformity of causal origin* between the bare secondary power or quality and its idea, there is no relation of *pattern* and *likeness* between them. What people usually take to be the real secondary quality is, in fact, only the idea of it present in the mind. This idea bears no resemblance to the real power in the thing and ceases to exist, once the perception itself ceases.

Locke states the contrast between primary and secondary qualities as that between *real, original* qualities and *imputed, sensible* ones. This way of expressing the difference is apt to be misleading, since by "imputed, sensible qualities," he means the *ideas* of secondary qualities which most people take to be the secondary qualities themselves. Locke does not deny the reality of secondary qualities, in his own meaning of the term. Bare powers do exist outside the sentient subject and do cause a set of its ideas, even though these ideas have no likeness to their causal sources. But he wants to emphasize that the heat, color, taste, and sound, which are ordinarily deemed to be "real qualities, existing right out there," are only the mental effects of bare powers, and that the powers themselves depend on the disposition and operation of the primary qualities. Since the ideas of secondary qualities have their entire formal reality in the percipient, they should not be attributed to the external thing. Locke also mentions a class of *tertiary qualities,* which are also bare powers in the thing resulting from the make-up of its primary qualities. Through its tertiary qualities, one body has the power so to change the texture of another body, that the latter will produce a new idea of a secondary quality in the observer's mind. Thus the sun has the power to affect wax in such a way that it takes on a different appearance, i.e., produces the idea of a different color in the person observing the change. Since tertiary qualities are also bare powers in bodies, they merely repeat, at one remove, the epistemological situation of the secondary qualities.

Significantly enough, Locke does not fully correlate his previous distinction between simple ideas of one sense and those of several senses with the present distinction between secondary and primary qualities. It is true that the simple ideas of one sense are — with but the single exception of the idea of solidity — ideas of bare powers or secondary qualities. But this single exception is of decisive importance. Although the *solidity* of bodies is revealed through the single sense of touch, it must be included as a primary quality, along with extension, figure, number, rest, and motion. The latter traits are all grasped through the co-operation of several senses, but they admit solidity to equal standing as a primary, original quality of real bodies. Here, Locke sides with Boyle and Newton, against the Cartesians. His inclusion of solidity in the list of primary qualities achieves a double purpose. First, it challenges the view of Hobbes and Descartes that primary qualities are objectively real only because they are reducible to extension and hence to exact mathematical description. Although Locke admires the demonstrative power of mathematical reasoning, he never seeks to measure either reality or the demonstrative process by an exclusively mathematical standard. Solidity is irreducible to extension and its modes, and yet is a primary aspect of bodies. Second, the fact that solidity is a real quality of bodies and yet is not reducible to extension and its modes is an argument against the Cartesian doctrine that extension is the special attribute of body and expresses its essence. Locke notes that solidity is just as indispensable as extension for bodily things. He displays a Newtonian reluctance to accept *res extensa* and *res cogitans* as truly essential definitions of body and mind.

Locke offers variations on the familiar Cartesian arguments in favor of the subjectivity of what men ordinarily take to be real, secondary qualities. He observes that water may seem hot to one hand and cold to the other, that the taste and color of an almond change upon its being pounded, that the color of a jewel changes with but a slight modification of the lighting conditions or the observer's perspective. He also stresses the connection between sensations of pain and pleasure and those of secondary qualities. The same bright fire produces comfortable warmth at a safe distance and intense pain at a closer distance. There is no stronger reason for locating the brightness and warmth in the fire itself than there is for locating the pain there. Berkeley's critique of primary qualities will take its start in these Lockean analyses. In Berkeley's estimation, his predecessor's theory is vulnerable on several scores. Locke passes unwarrantedly from saying that the ideas of qualities are caused in us, to saying that we know them to be caused in us precisely by distinct, subsistent, material things. Furthermore, he fails to clarify the sense in which the ideas of primary qualities are "like" the existing primary qualities, since he regards them as having another mode of being. Again, the close association between the bare powers or secondary qualities and the real primary qualities casts suspicion upon the knowability and objectivity of the latter. Finally, the subjective character of even the primary qualities is suggested by the fact that the primary quality of solidity is given through the same sense of touch which, admittedly, centers mainly upon the states of the perceiver. Berkeley readily exploits these openings in favor of his own immaterialism.

2. *Ideas of Substances.* These ideas are naturally aroused in the mind, because of two traits observable in our perception of particular modes of sensation or reflection. (*a*) The various modes are usually perceived as *belonging together* in different groups. To the qualities so united in a complex idea, we give the name of a single thing and then proceed to forget about its origin as a complex idea. (*b*) Moreover, the qualities so associated are regarded precisely *as modes,* since we cannot imagine them as having that ability to subsist of themselves which is characteristic of things. Consequently, the mind demands a principle sufficient to account for the coexistence of the modes as one thing, and to assure the thing's subsistent existence, as the support of the modes. The mind thus accustoms itself to suppose a unifying source and support of the complexus of modes. The complex idea of a particular substance is nothing more than this *customary supposition* of a substrate or unifying subject for a certain combination of simple ideas. The red color, sweet taste, peculiar texture, and shape of a cherry are modal ideas, united as one thing, and not themselves capable of independent existence. They carry with them the note of inherence or being supported, and hence they generate the idea of a subject or support. Since the relation of being supported cannot be founded in nothing, the mind conceives the vague but proportionate idea of a "something," which upholds these qualities and unites them in one thing.

If the mind tries to abstract from the ideas of particular substances a *general idea of substance* as such, it is left with "only an uncertain supposition of we know not what" support for the powers which produce simple ideas in us.[17] Sensation and reflection show a need

[17] *An Essay concerning Human Understanding,* I, iii, 19 (Fraser, I, 107). Despite this tenuous definition of substance in general, Locke remained a firm believer in the

for particular, material and spiritual substances to exist, but these experiential sources tell nothing about the nature of substance as such. Our minds reach only as far as the qualities and powers which produce our ideas of qualities; any real, underlying support of these qualities and powers remains supposed but unknown. The idea of substance as such resolves itself into a vague, obscure, and indistinct notion of a *something,* which bears the *relation of a support* to powers and is not itself upheld by anything else. The notion of a something or being is too general and indeterminate to give specific knowledge about substantial essence; the relational note suggests that our idea of substance is not of what it *is,* but only of what it *does.* Hence it is futile to search after the general nature of substantial essence: philosophy must restrict itself to modal ideas of particular substances. Locke comes upon no Cartesian special attribute that would give the mind any insight into the nature of either material or spiritual substance as such.

The line followed by Locke's empirical successors is adumbrated by his own analysis. Berkeley and Hume will agree that he is not being cautious enough even in restricting our knowledge to the ideas of particular substances, material and immaterial. Berkeley will challenge the need to make any transition from ideas of qualities to supposed real qualities, existing outside the mind and *in* some material subject. His contention will be that all the qualities *are* ideas and that, therefore, the only substrate we are forced to suppose is the mind itself or *immaterial* substance. As for Hume, he will inquire further into what it means to be *forced by custom to suppose* a substrate or substantial support. If the individual ideas of modes are distinct mental entities, the only ground for such compulsory supposition is a mental one, arising from habitual association. In that case, an empirical explanation can be given of our ideas of both immaterial and material substances, without having recourse to *any* real substantial beings, material or immaterial.

3. *Cause and Effect.* The lineaments of Hume's radical critique

existence of real particular substances. It was this belief that prevented him from taking a radically relational and phenomenalistic view of knowledge, to which his emphasis upon perceiving the relations among ideas might otherwise have led him. The role of substance, in keeping Locke halfway between a substantialist realism and radical phenomenalism, is described by J. Dewey, "Substance, Power and Quality in Locke," *Freedom and Experience,* edited by S. Hook and M. R. Convitz (Ithaca, Cornell University Press, 1947), 205–220.

of causality are also discernible in the Lockean handling of the ideas of cause and effect. Locke himself holds in check the implications of his phenomenalistic treatment of these ideas, because of his strong realistic conviction about actual causal transactions. The whole fabric of his philosophy supposes the reality of causal operations, without which the real existence of qualities, finite substances, and God cannot be proved.

Locke concentrates attention upon efficient cause, since this is the only one obtainable through a direct analysis of ideas. The empirical origin is found in the experience of *alteration among ideas,* such that there is a beginning of new ideas. Change of ideas of modes and substances is observable by both sense and reflection. An idea of a sense quality comes to be, whereas before it was not present in the mind; collections of modes are seen to be altered by some beginning; a new thought or act of volition makes its appearance. Such beginnings among ideas point to operations going on, and operations point to the ideas of active and passive powers. When applied in act, the active power is a *cause;* the motion received in the passive power, through operation, is an *effect.* Hence operations and powers supply the middle term between observed beginnings and the relation of cause and effect. The *causal principle* states that "everything that has a beginning must have a cause."[18] The cause is that which operates to produce any simple or complex idea, whereas the effect is that idea which is produced. The cause makes another thing begin to be; that which does have its being from the application of an operating power of another thing, is the effect. Cause may even be extended to include the substance, in which the active power is supposed to reside, although we can gain no knowledge of how the substance exerts causal action.

Although Locke's analysis rests upon observed cases of change, these instances belong entirely to the *field of ideas.* He does not begin with real changes transpiring in the sensible world, and hence he does not employ the Aristotelian distinction of act and potency, in the elucidation of the causal relation. His active and passive

---

[18] *First Letter to Stillingfleet,* quoted in Fraser, I, 433, n. 1. Another formulation, given in conjunction with the proof of God's existence, reads: "Nonentity cannot produce any real being . . . and what had a beginning must be produced by something else." *An Essay concerning Human Understanding,* IV, x, 3 (Fraser, II, 308). For Locke's formal analysis of power and cause, see *ibid.,* II, xxi, 1–5; xxvi, 1 (Fraser, I, 308–314, 433–434).

powers, in the first instance, bear reference to actual states of ideas. Since the change under description involves the displacement of one already-constituted idea or mental state by another, there is no opportunity for interpreting the change as the actualization of a real, natural potency. Nevertheless, Locke is not content to let the analysis remain only within the realm of ideas. His examination of alteration among ideas is intended to lead to the affirmation of real causal agents and operations.

The inference from operation upon perceivable ideas to real causal powers is conditioned, however, by the limits of experience. Locke has no doubt that observable change leads the mind to real effects and, in most instances, to a *passive power,* or stable capacity to receive similar changes in the future. But he encounters difficulty in respect to the real *active power* or cause. Undeniably, the mind is under compulsion to look for the cause, in each case of observed change. But whence comes the idea of an active power? There are two main classes of action: *motion* (communication of local change by bodily impulse) and *thinking. Bodies* cannot inform us about an active power involved in either sort of action. The behavior of bodies tells us nothing about the thinking process. Nor can bodies inform us about the formal beginning of motion, i.e., about the putting of oneself into action by one's own power. A body at rest conveys no such information, surely, whereas a body in motion tells us only about the passion or reception of communicated motion, not about the action or communicating of motion as such. Sense perception reaches only to the *transfer* of motion (as in the case of colliding billiard balls), not to its *production* by an active power. Sensation reveals only sequences of change and results of action, rather than the beginning of action or application of active power. For obtaining the latter idea, *reflection* is the sole empirical source. Even here, thought is a passive power, insofar as it is operating under the influence of outside sources. Only in acts of remembering, combining, and relating ideas, as well as in voluntary decisions to move one's bodily members, are the beginnings of action genuinely given in experience. Reflection upon these actions gives rise to the idea of cause or active causal power.

The upshot of Locke's investigation is that the idea of cause is grounded solely in reflection, and gets only an obscure and implicit support from sensation. This raises the question of whether cause and effect can ever be applied validly to the material world or to any other context than the production of ideas and voluntary states. The transition from ideal to real causation is not adequately made by Locke. Hume will want to know what sort of an anomaly is presented by the idea of an active power, which is founded in reflection and which cannot be traced back, with any determinate evidence, to sensation. Either reflection is an *independent source* of objectively valid ideas (and then sensation loses its primacy among the sources of experience) or else the idea of cause is traceable solely to *mental conditions* and does not apply to real things, as far as empirical knowledge is concerned. Unwittingly, Locke has prepared the way for Hume's own position on substance and cause, by giving a reason why our mind is unable to imagine a mode without a substance or a beginning of change without a cause. He notes that chance and the force of habit often alter our judgments, without our notice. Such ideas as mode and support, beginning of change and active power, are often joined together inadvertently and yet indissolubly, under the pressure of *fancy* or *the imaginative association of ideas*. Locke, to be sure, does not make a universal principle of explanation out of this observation. He even regards the association of ideas apart from the natural order of connection, as a kind of madness: it is the generative source of insanity, fanaticism, and bad reasoning. It is left for Hume to maintain that the association of ideas is the same as the natural order of connection (as far as empirical knowledge goes), and that the associative bonds are the source of whatever sanity, moderation, and good reasoning the human race possesses. Whereas Locke regards the compulsions of imagination as something of an aberration. Hume hails them as the very principles of stability and intelligibility in our view of the world of fact.

4. *Personal Identity*. Locke begins this inquiry by defining identity in a special way and by distinguishing various types of identity.[19] Following his "way of ideas," he settles the manner in which a being may be compared with itself, by giving a description of how the *idea of identity* arises. This idea applies to all things (whether substances or modes) which have their existence in place and time. The *principle of individuation* is existence itself, since it is in virtue of its existence that a being enjoys undisturbed its own time and place, to the exclusion of other beings of the same kind. A thing is known to be its own selfsame being by reason of our knowing it

---

[19] *Ibid.*, II, xxvii (Fraser, 439–470).

to exist somewhere at some time. The understanding can then compare its ideas about the thing, as presently existing, with ideas concerning its former existence. If these ideas are seen *not* to vary, the thing is known as identical with itself. The idea of identity is not used univocally but is applied to different kinds of things, according to their different ways of existing. Thus an inorganic thing is the same only as long as the same mass of atoms or body is present. But a living thing is self-identical in virtue of a continuous organization of parts, permitting participation in the same life, even though the particles of matter may be completely changed. Like the ideas about other animals, the idea about a man remains selfsame by reference to the same organized body and continued life, not merely in virtue of the idea about the same soul or thinking being.

Descartes had distinguished between the man and the self, regarding the former as the composite of mind and body and the latter as the thinking thing alone. Locke also is careful to distinguish between the man and the self, but in neither case does his meaning coincide with the Cartesian one. Since he does not recognize special attributes telling us about the nature of substances, he does not infer the necessary presence of two substances in man from the admitted presence of both thought and extension in him. Although it is quite likely that both material and spiritual substances are found in man, this opinion is only probable. It involves no contradiction to suppose that God might endow material substance with the power of thinking. Hence Locke's cautious conclusion about the idea of *the man* is that it must include ideas of a bodily substance and a thinking principle, the latter being *probably* a distinct, immaterial substance, rather than a function of the material substance. In any case, the sameness of an organized bodily life is indispensable for establishing the identity of the man.

Locke denies the Cartesian assumption that the problem of the identity of *the self* must be solved in terms of substance. The unity of material substance does not explain how plants and animals retain their identity, nor does the unity of a thinking spiritual substance explain the abiding identity of a man. A thinking being is a self, in virtue of the *consciousness* that always accompanies the thinking operation. It is a self to itself here and now, because of its consciousness of its present thoughts and actions. This provides a ground for the comparison of identity between the consciousness of past thoughts and actions and the consciousness of present thoughts and actions. There is an abiding personal identity, only insofar as this comparison can be made. Where conscious comparison trails off, there the personal identity also ends.

This psychological approach to personal identity remains independent of the question whether several substances share the same consciousness or whether the same substance enjoys several distinct consciousnesses. Locke thinks it more probable that a single, conscious self accompanies a single, spiritual substance, but he does not rule out the other possibilities. He could welcome later psychological findings about multiple and alternating personalities. It is largely through Locke that the problem of personal selfhood became divorced from that of the substantial nature of man. This development is an indication of the bankruptcy of the Cartesian theory of substance. But in cutting off his notion of personal identity from any ontological basis and making it solely an affair of comparative acts of consciousness, Locke is left with *three separate sorts of identity:* that of the substance, that of the man, and that of the person or self. He does not explain how the identity of the self can be that of *one human person,* smacking always of "a tang of the cask."[20] The three identities disrupt the unity and selfsameness of the single human person of our experience. The analytic way of ideas does not fully account for the unity of human experience.

6. ABSTRACTION OF GENERAL IDEAS

Instead of proceeding directly from the study of various kinds of ideas to the problem of knowledge proper, Locke first examines how ideas are abstracted and rendered universal. If men limited themselves to particular ideas and names, the process of discovery and communication would be rendered endless and uselessly complicated. Actually, we are able to form general ideas and words, which are of incalculable advantage for the advancement of knowledge. *Words* as such are the sensible marks or signs of ideas. Their proper and immediate signification is only of the *ideas in one's own mind,* and it is a perversion to obscure this basic reference. Nevertheless, the mind naturally tends to regard words also as standing for real things and for the common meanings of ideas in other minds. Especially in the use of general words, we often forget the primary

---

[20] *An Essay concerning Human Understanding,* II, i, 17 (Fraser, 136). Read H. E. Allison, "Locke's Theory of Personal Identity: A Re-examination," *Journal of the History of Ideas,* 27 (1966), 41–58.

reference of words to our own ideas and hence relate them immediately to things. As a counterbalance, Locke sometimes says that words refer to *nothing but* one's own ideas. He does strive, however, to establish an ultimate reference to the real order of things and common meanings.

Against Hobbes' nominalism, Locke maintains the distinction between ideas and words or sounds. The latter are only the signs of the former. Since all existent things are particular beings, our original ideas are particular ones, having particular names. But we are led to generalize our ideas under the pressure of various considerations: the limits of memory, the infinite number of particular existents, and the requirements of research and social intercourse. Locke gives both a psychological and a logical account of the *process of generalization of ideas,* whence general names result.[21]

Psychologically considered, the child's first ideas and words are the particular ones which refer to the most important individuals in his narrow sphere of life. Gradually, his experience widens to the point where he notices certain resemblances between, say, his father or mother and other individuals. All these individuals agree in shape and some other qualities, which agreement persists, despite obvious differences on other points. The common aspects are used to frame the general idea, which carries the name "man." What has been done is to leave out of account the peculiarities involved in the complex idea of one's father, and retain only the traits which observation shows to be shared by many other individuals. Nothing new has been added to the particular complex ideas of various individual men, but a new complex idea has been formed by combining only the *jointly shared* notes. The fresh idea is a general one, to which is given (or accepted from conventional usage) a distinctive, general name. This abstracted, general idea, along with its name, is then laid up in memory precisely as containing the essence of a sort or *species* of thing. It is presumed that all knowledge gained about this species is rightfully applicable to all individuals in the class.

A *logical* justification is demanded, however, for the presumption that the abstract idea expresses a universal species and is predicable of a certain group of individuals. With what right does the understanding bind its particular ideas together in bundles and rank them in classes? In reply, Locke appeals to two relevant operations of the

---

21 *An Essay concerning Human Understanding,* III, iii, 6–11 (Fraser, II, 16–22); cf. II, xi, 9; IV, iii, 31; vii, 9 (Fraser, I, 206–207; II, 224–225, 274).

mind: separating and relating. The process of *separating* or *abstracting* isolates an idea from its experiential context and from the other ideas originally accompanying it. Since existence under the conditions of place and time constitutes the principle of individuation, abstraction is primarily a removal from the concrete conditions of existence. A certain idea is separated from the particular setting of place and time, and is regarded as a bare appearance or isolated unit of meaning. So abstracted, the idea becomes capable of representing more than one individual. It is now a general representative, constituting a genus or species, and its name becomes applicable to all those individual existents which *show a conformity* with this idea. Their conformity gives them the right to be classified under this genus or species, and to receive its name. General ideas are thus erected into standards, by reference to which the various individuals can be arranged and analyzed for practical and scientific purposes.

Nevertheless, an explanation in terms of separating or abstracting cannot yield the full solution of the problem of universal ideas. For, since nothing is added to the particular complex idea in forming the universal, it follows that the abstracted idea also remains *particular*. After omissions are made, the remainder is still a particular idea or complexus of ideas, in which a number of individuals are found to agree. This leads Locke to inquire how one particular idea or set of ideas, even taken in separation from other circumstances, can stand for a number of singular existents. He is obliged to specify more definitely the manner in which the general idea is "framed and set up," precisely *as a representative*. Taking advantage of the Cartesian distinction between the formal and objective reality of ideas, he distinguishes between the *formal existence* of the abstracted idea and its *objective signification*. The former aspect remains particular, whereas the latter becomes general. The meaning of an idea is rendered general by means of the second relevant operation of the mind: *relating*. The general meaning of ideas is "nothing but the capacity they are put into, by the understanding, of signifying or representing many particulars. For the signification they have is nothing but a relation that, by the mind of man, is added to them."[22]

To the extent that they are general in meaning or signification, ideas are *products of the understanding,* considered as a relating

---

[22] *Ibid.,* III, iii, 11 (Fraser, II, 22). On Locke's use of a current biological model of classification, cf. D. A. Givner, "Scientific Preconceptions in Locke's Philosophy of Language," *Journal of the History of Ideas,* 23 (1962), 340–354.

function. Locke emphasizes that the relation of signifying many
particulars is added by the mind, so that he can overcome the tendency
to attribute real existence to genera and species. Only individual
things are really existent; general meanings are the workmanship of
the mind and have their being only in the mind. Still, Locke is not
entirely satisfied with this conceptualistic position, since he observes
that the mental function of relating and generalizing is guided by
certain deliverances of experience. He expresses his belief that "nature"
has made things *alike* in certain respects. Hence the mind puts
into a certain idea the capacity of signifying many particulars, only
because of the testimony of sense to the presence of a likeness or
similar set of sensible qualities, in a number of individual existents.
This perceived likeness is the ultimate regulator of the abstraction of
certain notes, the generalization of their signification, and their
application to rightful members of the species.

Locke's precarious balance between the contribution of sense perception and the mental operations of separating-and-relating tends
to get upset, however, as soon as he considers particular instances of
general ideas. The difficulties crop up when he inspects mathematical
ideas and the species of natural substances.

> For, when we nicely reflect upon them, we shall find that *general
> ideas* are fictions and contrivances of the mind, that carry difficulty with
> them, and do not so easily offer themselves as we are apt to imagine.
> For example, does it not require some pains and skill to form the
> general idea of a triangle (which is yet none of the most abstract, com-
> prehensive, and difficult) for it must be neither oblique nor rectangle,
> neither equilateral, equicrural, nor scalenon; but all and none of these
> at once. In effect, it is something imperfect, that cannot exist; an idea
> wherein some parts of several different and inconsistent ideas are put
> together.[23]

As for the species of natural substances, Locke is guided by the
requirements of his method and doctrine on the knowledge of
substances, on the one side, and certain experimental procedures,
on the other. The chemist continues to call a substance sulphur
or vitriol, even though it displays quite different sets of properties,
under different experimental conditions. Locke reasons that, if the
definition of the chemical species involved the real substantial essence,
then there could not be such a shift of sensible appearances from one
experimental situation to another. Hence the specific definition of
things does not express the real substantial essence in any way, but is

---

[23] *An Essay concerning Human Understanding,* IV, vii, 9 (Fraser, II, 274).

solely concerned with the nominal essence. This *nominal essence* is an artificial construction of the logical genus and species, based upon the sensible qualities alone. It is not governed by the inner, substantial constitution of the thing or its *real essence*. This accords with Locke's methodological limitation to a description in terms of ideas, as well as with his general denial that the human mind can know the nature of real substances. The effect of such particular analyses is to stress the "fictitious" and "contrived" character of general ideas, and to render their real foundation in experience extremely insecure.

There are several tangled skeins of reasoning in Locke's doctrine on general ideas. (1) He opposes Hobbesian nominalism by distinguishing between ideas and names, and by admitting the existence of general ideas, of which general names are only the signs. (2) He also opposes any extreme view that would accord real existence to our generic and specific notions. Locke firmly respects the realistic theses that only individual things can exist and that the mind itself contributes the formal universality of signification. (3) But Locke's historical, plain method falters in the explanation of the foundation of generality of meaning. The two operations of separating and relating are not radical enough principles to save the real ground of reference for general meanings. The process of separation or abstraction can work, only when the mind is in possession of some selective basis for determining *which* ideas are capable of isolation and also capable of combination with each other in a complex general idea. Similarly, the relating process can establish generality of meaning, only on condition that the mind has some guidance about *which* things can find in a certain idea their common representative. In a word, the operations of abstracting and relating, as described by Locke, *presuppose* the apprehension of similarities as such. But such an apprehension does issue in a distinctively general idea, that is not reducible to an isolated segment of our particular images. For, the abstractive process is not just a separating and bundling of particulars, but a penetration to the essential structure.

(4) Locke himself hints at the real foundation for general meanings, when he remarks that "nature" makes things to be alike and that things display an intrinsic conformity with the general idea. These observations are only a hair's breadth removed from granting that there is an intellectual apprehension of the real, substantial essence. But the admission is never made. This failure is due, in part, to Locke's ingrained suspicion of any distinctively intellectual apprehen-

sion. For, he has in mind the Cartesian and Cambridge Platonist claims to a "purely intellectual act," which operates apart from, and often in opposition to, sensory perception. Another reason for Locke's reluctance to push the analysis any deeper, is that his "way of ideas" prevents him from passing from supposition of the factual existence of substances to knowledge of their essential nature. As a consequence of this methodological limitation, however, he can speak only metaphorically about "nature's way" of making things alike. He is defenseless before Hume's emendation, which maintains that by "nature" is meant only the customary drift of our thoughts, rather than a real participation of things in a similarity of essence. Locke's opportunity to escape this Humean consequence comes with his recognition of an intrinsic conformity of things with their general idea, giving them the right to be classified in one determinate species. But his phenomenalism requires him to interpret this conformity entirely in terms of the sensible qualities themselves. Instead of *manifesting* something about the real substantial essence, the determinate combination of sense qualities *constitutes* the nominal essence or definition by means of genus and specific difference. Hence the likeness among many individuals and the determinate structure of conformity, within the sensible thing, are never connected with the real, substantial essence, in howsoever indirect a way.

(5) Locke's particular analyses of the idea of a triangle and that of a physical substance, like sulphur, are specially illuminating. Locke admits a difference between mathematical and physical abstraction, but it is one of degree and not of kind. His difficulty in respect to the object of mathematical abstraction arises from his failure to distinguish between the composite image of a sort of common-denominator triangle and the concept of triangle. The particularity of his "general idea of *a* triangle," which must be "all and none" of the several types of triangles at once, leads to a noetic monstrosity. One can sympathize with Berkeley's despair of making any sense out of abstract ideas of this sort. Perhaps more significant for the general direction of modern thought, however, are Locke's animadversions concerning real essences and their relationship with scientific research. On two scores, his approach is typical of the subsequent handling of this issue by empiricists. (*a*) He makes no distinction between the meaning of "species" in metaphysics and in the natural sciences. Because the scientific conception of a species is often only a tool for classification and nominal definition, he concludes that the human

mind is *always* confined to the nominal essence. (*b*) He identifies all philosophical views of the real, substantial essence with that of Cartesian rationalism. Since the extravagant claims of rationalism to have an adequate understanding of the essence of material substance and to use that as a guiding principle in scientific demonstration cannot be confirmed by the actual condition of our knowledge, Locke rules out *any* grasp of the real essence. He is right in stressing the fragmentary and superficial state of so much of our knowledge, as well as the presence of contingent events and monstrosities in nature. But this evidence is decisive only against an extreme claim to essential insight and against a natural philosophy that rules out the distinctively material or potential principle in natural things. Somewhere between these extremes of rationalism and phenomenalism, there is room for the realistic claim that the human mind can gain a minimal, essential knowledge of at least the nature of man and the broad division between the living and the nonliving. The limitations of human intelligence and the relative opacity of material things prevent us from having a perfect vision of the structures of material things, and recommend the cultivation of the various scientific techniques of descriptive analysis. As Locke formulates it, the problem of species is a misleading one, since it consolidates a number of issues that should be kept distinct.

7. THE STRUCTURE OF KNOWLEDGE

There are two major areas of tension in Locke's theory of knowledge which urgently call for some sort of resolution. The first polarity is between the *analytic* and *synthetic* tendencies in his thought. His chosen method is basically an analytic, elementaristic one, laying stress upon the atomic units of our mental life. But there is an equally strong need to reunite the analyzed elements in a unified knowledge, achieved through intellectual *perception* or the mental act of grasping the bonds among ideas. Locke reinterprets the traditional maxim about knowledge being found in the judgment to mean that it is found most properly in *judging as an act* reducible to mental perception. However, *judgment as a special faculty* does not yield knowledge but probable assent. Perception or the act of judging is the proper locus of knowledge, and the analysis of ideas is only preliminary to it. Once innatism is eliminated, Locke allows the mind's teleology for unified knowledge. The second tension concerns Locke's previous teaching that the idea is the mind's immediate object. Now he must admit that the mind is also oriented mediately toward an apprehension of real being. A way must be found, then, to reconcile the *immediate* and the *mediate* objects of our understanding. The fourth book of the *Essay* seeks to bind these various contrasts together in a coherent doctrine about the nature, degrees, extent, and reality of human knowledge.

1. The point of departure is the definition of the *nature* of knowledge as:

> *The perception of the connexion and agreement, or disagreement and repugnancy, of any of our ideas.* In this alone it consists. Where this perception is, there is knowledge, and where it is not, there, though we may fancy, guess, or believe, yet we always come short of knowledge.[24]

This definition conforms with the basic premise that the understanding is concerned directly with its own ideas and their various bonds. The various types of perception depend upon the various relations of agreement or disagreement among ideas. Locke reduces these to four kinds: identity and diversity, relation, coexistence and necessary connection, and real existence. The perception of *identity* and *diversity* is called the first act of the mind in the order of knowing, since it is concomitant with the mental possession of any idea. In having any idea, the understanding grasps it precisely as being what it is (identity) and as distinct from every other idea (diversity). Relation and coexistence are both instances of relation, in the broader sense. But Locke establishes a sharp epistemological distinction between abstract, purely mental connections and concrete ones, grounded in a real subject (a distinction which Hume reformulated as the pivotal one between ideal relations and relations among matters of fact). Hence he restricts *relation,* in the stricter sense, to perception of agreement or disagreement among ideas only, whereas *coexistence* bears upon the mutual presence of qualities in the same real subject. Finally, there is a distinct sort of agreement whereby the mind gains knowl-

---

[24] *Ibid.,* IV, i, 2 (Fraser, II, 167–168). In his critical study, "Some Points in the Philosophy of Locke," *Philosophy,* 12 (1937), 33–46, A. C. Ewing observes that, in terms of this definition, the object of knowledge is shifted from *ideas* to the *relations among ideas.* In order to accommodate knowledge of real existents, however, Locke is forced subsequently to expand the meaning of knowledge still further, from a grasp of relations solely among ideas to include a grasp of relations between our *ideas* and *real existents.* That he relies implicitly upon an ontological (not solely a logical and psychological) theory of signs is shown by R. I. Armstrong, "John Locke's 'Doctrine of Signs': A New Metaphysics," *Journal of the History of Ideas,* 26 (1965), 369–382, and by F. Costa, "Instances transcendantales dans la 'théorie des signes' de Locke," *Revue de Métaphysique et de Morale,* 63 (1958), 202–232.

edge of *real existence,* from an examination of certain ideas.

2. The *degrees* of knowledge are: intuition, demonstration, and sensation. Locke describes the first two degrees mainly in the Cartesian spirit. *Intuition* consists in an immediate perception of the agreement or disagreement among ideas, which are seen together at first sight and without the intervention of any other ideas. The difference between a circle and a triangle is at once evident, requiring no intermediate connections and inferences. *"It is on this intuition that depends all the certainty and evidence of all our knowledge.* . . . A man cannot conceive himself capable of a greater certainty than to know that any idea in his mind is such as he perceives it to be; and that two ideas, wherein he perceives a difference, are different and not precisely the same."[25] *Demonstration* or reasoning is a process of supplying the intervening links required in order to join together two ideas, which originally stood in no immediate connection. In demonstrative knowledge, the agreement or disagreement is perceived through the mediation of other ideas.

Like Descartes, Locke requires that every stage in the demonstration be itself secured by an intuitive perception, and that these intermediate intuitions be kept in mind throughout the inference. Both thinkers also agree in emphasizing the difficulties of reasoning, which requires considerable attention, memory, and perseverance, in order to carry out all the required steps. These conditions tend to weaken the clarity and force of the connection, especially by comparison with a simple intuition. Locke departs from Descartes, however, on several particulars. *Doubt* functions only as a prelude to demonstration and does not touch the immediate intuitions, mathematical or otherwise. And although he demands an intuition at each step in demonstration, as well as a memory of previous intuitions, Locke does not aim at a quasi-intuition of the entire course of the demonstration. Locke does not provide *memory* with any divine guarantee but appeals to our ability to form abstract, general ideas and to demonstrate general truths. It may be safely presumed that general connections, once demonstrated, will remain self-identical and true, forever. Finally, the Cartesian predilection for mathematical demonstration is criticized. What makes *mathematical reasoning* demonstrative is no special feature associated

[25] *An Essay concerning Human Understanding,* IV, ii, 1 (Fraser, II, 177–178). For a documented report on Locke's close knowledge of Descartes and the Cartesians, see C. S. Ware, "The Influence of Descartes on John Locke. A Bibliographical Study," *Revue Internationale de Philosophie,* 4 (1950), 210–230; this article is based upon papers in the Lovelace Collection (mentioned in the bibliography to this chapter).

with extension, figure, and number, but only a ready perception of the agreement or disagreement among such ideas. Numbers and geometrical figures are precise and steady symbols, which therefore aid discourse and memory. But there is no intrinsic reason for making a prototype out of mathematical procedures, since nonmathematical ideas (especially moral ones) also have determinate relations of agreement and disagreement which can, in principle, be discovered by a proper method. The essential factor in demonstration is *not the nature of the formal object* but the *evidence of the connection* among ideas. Locke does admit that the demonstrative rigor of even moral philosophy would be increased through the use of mathematical symbols and method. Unlike Leibniz, however, he makes no definite attempt to treat moral problems mathematically.

Locke's own account of knowledge, as a perception of ideal connections, would seem to limit the kinds of knowledge to intuition and demonstration about *ideas*. But the empirical fact is that I am certain of the existence of this *thing,* here and now affecting my senses. To accommodate this fact, a distinction is made between the degrees of *general knowledge* (intuition and demonstration, as described) and sensation as a *particular knowledge* of individual, finite existents. This particular, existential knowledge holds an anomalous position, somewhere midway between mere probability and the full certainty of intuition and demonstration.[26] *Sensation,* as knowledge, consists in an awareness of the actual entrance of ideas from sensible existents. Locke speaks loosely about perceiving the existence of particular things, through this means. More accurately, he can only claim that one perceives certain ideas, precisely as being received here and now from an actually operating, causal source. To grasp the existential act of another thing, in an existential judgment, would sap the foundations of the Lockean method of ideas. But he allows that there can be practical assurance of the existing reality of the particular source of some ideas, especially those that are accompanied by pleasure or pain. Locke locates this pragmatic conviction between probability and certainty, so that there may be guidance in the practical conduct of life.

3. It is now possible to determine the exact *extent* of human knowledge.[27] It can extend no farther than we have ideas and,

---

[26] *An Essay concerning Human Understanding,* IV, ii, 14 (Fraser, II, 185–188).

[27] *Ibid.,* IV, iii (Fraser, II, 190–225). Robert Boyle's tempering influence is noticeable here; cf. G. A. J. Rogers, "Boyle, Locke, and Reason," *Journal of the History of Ideas,* 27 (1966), 205–216.

indeed, no farther than we can perceive *connections* among our ideas. There are various ways of gauging the extent of knowledge, one of which is provided by the theory of the degrees of knowledge. From the mind's need to employ reasoning, it is evident that we do not have intuitive knowledge of all the agreements and disagreements among ideas. Furthermore, it is not always possible to find the middle terms linking ideas together, so that demonstrative knowledge can be acquired. Finally, sensitive knowledge is circumscribed even more severely than intuition and demonstration, since it is confined to particular, sensible things, existing here and now. Locke draws the modest conclusion that our knowledge not only falls short of the great expanse of real being which exists beyond the limits of "this little canton," our solar system, but is also of lesser extent than our ideas. Although clear and distinct ideas are requisite for knowledge, they are not — as Descartes held — sufficient criteria for acquiring knowledge of objects beyond their own self-identity and mutual diversity.

Another way of determining the scope of knowledge is provided by the various kinds of agreement and disagreement. We can know intuitively that every idea in the mind is one with its own content and distinct from every other idea. Hence there is intuitive knowledge of the self-identity and diversity of all our ideas. But it is difficult to determine beforehand the extent of our knowledge of *abstract* relations, since the mind is self-reliant in determining purely ideal connections. Locke sets no a priori limit to our ability to construct and relate purely ideal entities. He contents himself with observing that demonstration is just as cogent in the field of moral relations as in that of quantitative ones.

In regard to the *concrete relations of coexistence,* however, Locke does venture to draw some rigid lines of demarcation for our knowledge of coexisting qualities. Relying heavily upon the attitude of Boyle, Newton, and the British scientific school, he specifies certain limits beyond which the mind cannot go, in principle, in the investigation of nature. Although we can have sensitive knowledge of the actual copresence of certain sense qualities that give content to our ideas of particular substances, we cannot convert this *contingent* kind of information into a general principle of *demonstration.* Hence we must abandon the Cartesian pretension to a rigorous science of bodies, based on essential knowledge and necessary connections. Locke is rationalist enough, however, to admit that a philosophy of nature *should* realize this deductive ideal of determining beforehand, and without trial, what further properties and operations of bodies may be expected. But in fact, the necessary connections and negative inferences that can be drawn from an analysis of the ideas of qualities, are too contingent and restricted to provide a foundation for an a priori science of nature.

Locke cites three major hindrances to the development of a Cartesian-like *natural philosophy,* in which reason would anticipate and transcend the findings of sense observation. First, our ideas of qualities do not convey a knowledge of the real essence of substances. Hence we remain ignorant of the supposed *root* from which the properties and operations flow. Second, our certitudinal knowledge of primary qualities is of a very general sort. We know that every body must have *some* degree of extension, solidity, figure, and other traits, but we have no purely rational way of determining the *precise* size, figure, and texture of the parts of any particular body. And Locke is pessimistic about the prospect of ever acquiring circumstantial knowledge of the "insensible parts" or minute, submicroscopic particles, upon the determination of which, nevertheless, our whole knowledge of bodies is ultimately dependent. Finally, he is able to discover in experience *no connection between primary and secondary qualities.* Hence no demonstration is possible in regard to the sensible qualities of bodies. This does not put an end to the advance of the sciences, but it does force them to rely heavily upon the intrinsically less perfect, but humanly more proportionate, means of *observation* and *experiment.* Our knowledge of immaterial substances is even more meager than that of material ones, since it is based solely upon an analogy with what we experience in our own internal operations of thinking and willing.

4. Because of its philosophical importance for later British empiricism, the *extent* of our knowledge of agreements and disagreements of *real existence* deserves separate consideration. Abstract ideas and general propositions inform us only about essences and ideal connections, not about factual existence. Nevertheless, the mind can have intuitive knowledge of its own existence, demonstrative knowledge of God's existence, and sensitive knowledge of the existence of other things.[28]

Locke does not follow Descartes in according a privileged, systematic

---

[28] *An Essay concerning Human Understanding,* IV, iii, 2; ix, 2-3; x, 1-11; xi, 1-10 (Fraser, II, 212, 304-316, 325-336).

place to the *intuition of the existing self*. He merely ranges this one existential intuition alongside of the various essential intuitions we have of ideal identities, diversities, and relations. Having given a psychological definition of personal self-identity, Locke is aware of no special problems in this area. No proof is needed, and little critical explanation is given, for the evident, internal perception that we are existent. If anyone doubts his own existence, in the face of his experience of thinking, willing, or feeling pain, Locke makes the Cartesian retort that doubting itself is an incontrovertible and immediate evidence of the self's existence. The self is presented, by concomitant awareness, in all our conscious entertainment of ideas. Locke gives no satisfactory account, however, of how the general theory of intuition, as an immediate perception of connections *among ideas,* is to be adapted to this situation, in which the perceived connection is between an *idea* and an *existent.* An explanation may perhaps be sought in the twofold way of looking at an idea: either as a content of meaning or as a particular, existing perfection. But then the problem is only pushed back a step, namely, to how the mind can pass from the idea regarded as a self-identical meaning to the idea regarded precisely as an existential perfection.

There is one sense, however, in which the intuition of the existing self does fill a special role in Locke's philosophy. *Demonstration of God's existence* must start from an intuitive and existential basis, which is provided only by the apprehension of one's own existence. I know intuitively that I actually exist and that my real being cannot be produced by nothing. It is demonstratively certain, from the fact of my real being and the force of the principle of causality, that something must have existed from eternity. This eternal being is either myself or, if I give evidence of having a beginning, some other being that is itself eternal and the cause of my coming to be. The changes and limits in my way of being indicate that I did have a beginning. This was due to the causal activity of a being, in whom there is at least as much perfection as is contained in myself and the rest of the world of things subject to a beginning. This eternal being is the first cause or God. He is an all-powerful, intelligent being, wholly immaterial, and the providential source of the unity and perfections in the visible world.

Locke considers this proof to be just as cogent as any mathematical demonstration, and more certain than knowledge of anything else existing outside oneself. Yet he makes no attempt to overhaul the *principle of causality,* so that it may be used in this instance. Since the principle itself is an abstract, general proposition, it may perhaps be confined to the ideal order of demonstration. And since the idea of an active, causal power has been traced to an empirical source only in reflection, some justification is needed to apply it to a transcendent and nonempirical reality. A more elaborate discussion of the logical foundation of the proof of God's existence is required. This is especially urgent, since Locke bases his rejection of the Cartesian, a priori argument on the double ground that the idea of the infinite has an empirical origin and that existential demonstration cannot be made from a purely ideal meaning. Locke should show in more detail that he has secured an existential and empirical starting point in the intuited self, and that the principle of causality can be used to infer (from this starting point) the existence of a supraempirical being. This line of criticism suggested itself naturally to Hume, upon examination of Locke's demonstration of God's existence.

The weakest sort of existential knowledge is that of things other than the self and God. There is neither intuition nor demonstration, but only *sensitive knowledge,* in the case of the *real existence of material things.* This knowledge is limited to individual cases, and obtains only while the existent source of ideas of sensation is here and now operative, in respect to my sense powers. Knowledge of past existence is only as strong as the memory of past reception of ideas. About the future reality of a material thing and its future influence on consciousness, only probable opinions can be advanced. The existence of other spiritual beings is matter for natural belief. But within this narrow compass, sensitive knowledge is adequate to the practical needs of life.

In defense of our conviction about a *real external world,* Locke makes several observations that have become common patrimony for most subsequent realists. That our senses do receive their ideas from a nonsubjective origin is suggested by the fact that, whenever one sense organ is lacking, the corresponding proper ideas are also lacking. Moreover, there are some ideas which we cannot avoid receiving, even though we might prefer to escape from them or declare them nonexistent. This is especially true in the case of perceptions accompanied by pain. We do not have them at our disposal, in the way in which we can control or dismiss our own mental creations. Although we may shrink from them, such perceptions impose their own presence upon us. Empirically considered, there is also a notable difference between receiving a painful perception and recalling that experience in the tranquillity of memory. Finally, Locke observes that the various senses tend to corroborate each other's report, thus providing us with reliable, convergent testimony that our certainty about existing things is no product of our own consciousness or fancy. To this extent, Locke maintains that we do perceive our ideas of sensation precisely as being received from an extramental causal source.

5. Briefly, the problem of the *reality* of knowledge is that of the agreement between ideas and things.[29] The entire tendency of the previous examination of aspects of knowledge has been to widen the definition of knowledge to include some kind of assurance about the connection between ideas and real things, as well as between one idea and another. With this revision in mind, Locke now makes a review of the various kinds of ideas. *Simple* ideas are naturally produced by existent things, operating upon the mind, in accordance with God's ordination. The ideas of primary and secondary qualities *conform with* the things from which they derive, even though the ideas of secondary qualities do not *bear a likeness to* their objective foundation in bare powers. *Complex* ideas (with the exception of substance) are not intended to be copies of independent things but are of our own making. Hence they are their own archetypes and need only be combined and related in consistent ways, in order to have reality and truth of a nonexistential sort. The *ideas of substances* are of an intermediate nature. Like other complex ideas, they are formed by the mind itself. Yet like simple ideas, they claim to conform with independent archetypes, existing outside the mind. Because of this existential reference, combined with the absence of any perceivable necessary connection among the ideas of primary and secondary qualities, the mere *mutual compatibility* among the various qualitative ideas, making up an idea of a substance, is not a sufficient criterion for determining that this is an idea of any really existing substance. Many ideal combinations among qualitative ideas can be made by the mind, but there is no a priori way of settling which combination refers to a really existing thing. Only that grouping of complex ideas which has *actually been drawn* from the existent thing, con-

29 *Ibid.*, IV, iv (Fraser, II, 226–243). Locke's interest in the reality question and the cautious use of physical and medical hypotheses is studied by L. Laudan, "The Nature and Sources of Locke's Views on Hypotheses," *Journal of the History of Ideas*, 28 (1967), 211–223.

stitutes a real idea of a substance, expressing a conformity with an existing archetype. How the connection can be traced from ideas, as instrumental signs, to the existent things signified by ideas, remains fundamentally unclarified by Locke.

This doctrine on the reality of knowledge contains an implicit rebuke of attempts to measure the real world by the scope of our knowledge. The conditions of an ideal science cannot be imposed upon real things. Neither can these conditions be imposed upon the human mind, making it discard all cognitions that do not meet the strict requirements for knowledge. There is plenty of room for probable views, especially in the fields of practical improvement and religion. Locke himself tried to advance the economic welfare of his country in quite empirical ways, through currency reforms and tedious economic studies. The practical effect of his religious outlook was *deistic,* since he made reason the final arbiter in religious matters. Although Locke restricted the competence of reason in natural philosophy, he tried to reduce Christian belief to its "reasonable" elements.[30] The foundations of religion are the purely natural demonstrations of God's existence and the moral law. For the rest, practically orientated, probable views must regulate religious, moral, and political life.

8.   PRACTICAL PHILOSOPHY

Since Locke originally devised his method for the resolution of practical problems, he transferred to this sphere his characteristic blending of confident rationalism and cautious empiricism. In principle, he claimed that moral science can be demonstrated just as stringently as mathematics. For, moral reasonings concern abstract relations among ideas, and hence fall within the domain where demonstrative certainty is obtainable. But Locke's own samples of ethical demonstrations were tautologous and trifling, so that for the most part he offered a compromise way of thinking, in moral as well as natural philosophy. He recognized that, in any practical

[30] C. J. O'Neil gives an affirmative answer to his question: "Is Locke's State the Secular State?" *The New Scholasticism,* 26 (1952), 424–440, in view of the fact that faith is reduced to reason, and charity to natural duty. For an appraisal of the influence of his religious position on the rest of Locke's philosophy, see J. T. Noonan, "The Protestant Philosophy of John Locke," *Philosophical Studies in Honor of The Very Reverend Ignatius Smith, O.P.,* edited by J. K. Ryan (Westminster, Md., The Newman Press, 1952), 92–126.

elaboration of an ethical doctrine, difficulties are presented by the complex and mixed character of ethical ideas, the vagueness of ethical language, and the special distractions of interest and the passions. Moreover, ethics would be a singularly ineffective and unreal science, if it were severed from all connection with existential grounds. Hence Locke related the content of morality to God on the one side, and to the actual operations of the self on the other.

Morality rests upon the *relation of human actions to law,* whether it be the law of God, of the civil community, or of private convention.[31] The demonstration of God's existence provides morality with an ultimate foundation. The true ground of morality is in the *will* and *law of God.* The will of God is the basis of moral law, but God's decrees are those of a reasonable agent. As a providential creator, God sets an eternal law for men to find and follow. This law is embodied in the nature of things and is discoverable by the unaided *natural light,* i.e., by sense and reason working together to grasp the practical import of particular facts and the permanent relations among general ideas. Finite beings are dependent upon God and owe Him their obedience and free service. Moral ideas of good and evil concern the *obligatory conformity* of our voluntary actions to rules, especially the natural law of the divine lawmaker.

From the standpoint of the human agent, however, *good* and *evil* can be defined in terms of the *pleasure* and *pain* produced by actions.[32] Locke tries to reconcile a natural-law and a hedonistic theory of morality. The great end of human action is the possession of happiness, a motive that can be made to serve the purposes of moral law. Morally good and evil deeds entail the consequences of pleasure and pain, attached by the lawmaker. God associates certain rewards or punishments with actions that stand, respectively, in conformity or disconformity with the moral law. Men are moved more forcefully by hedonistic considerations than by reflection upon rational relations and obligation, but both routes provide a natural guide to right action. Under optimum conditions, reason should regulate self-interest, and

[31] *Draft A of An Essay concerning Human Understanding,* 26 (edited by R. I. Aaron and J. Gibb, 39); *Excerpts from Journals for April 3 and June 26, 1681* (Aaron and Gibb, 114–116); *An Essay concerning Human Understanding,* II, xxviii, 7–14 (Fraser, I, 475–480); *The Second Treatise of Civil Government,* II, 6, 8 (*Two Treatises of Government,* edited by T. I. Cook, 123, 124). See Locke's *Essays on the Law of Nature,* and J. W. Yolton's "Locke on the Law of Nature," *The Philosophical Review,* 67 (1958), 477–498.

[32] *An Essay concerning Human Understanding,* II, xx, 2–3; xxi, 63; xxviii, 5 (Fraser, I, 303–356, 474).

the latter should assure the practical application of general precepts to the individual and social search after happiness. The morally good man will recognize his obligation to conform with the moral law, as well as the advantages accruing from such virtuous conduct.

In underlining the role of God's *will* as the determinant of the eternal law, Locke reflected the voluntarist influence upon moral philosophy. Descartes had combined this emphasis with a confidence in the ability of reason to furnish practical guidance and to elaborate a moral philosophy. But Locke's appeal to the natural light of reason, as a means for discovering the law of God, did not have the same force as the similarly worded appeal made by Descartes and the Cambridge Platonists. For, he rejected their metaphysical explanations of the relation between God and the human mind, without providing a specific theory of his own. Hence his conception of "reason," as a guide in moral life, was a quite pliable standard. In respect to problems of individual and social morality, it tended to mean the prevailing views of his own age and social group.

In what sense is the individual free to act for or against moral ends? Locke declared the question of the *freedom* of *the will* to be strictly nonsensical, since freedom is one power and will another.[33] The one power cannot be predicated of the other, but both belong to the man or concrete subject exercising these powers. Will is an ability to determine our thought and preference in regard to a course of action, whereas liberty is an ability to do an action which we have chosen or willed. Hence the only authentic question concerns whether *the man* is free. He is certainly free to do what he wills (and so much, Hobbes admits), but it is not so clear that he is also free in respect to willing itself. At first, Locke followed the opinion that the will is always determined by the greater positive good. But further analysis disclosed that, although good and evil do work upon the agent, what immediately determines the will is some uneasiness or desire for an absent good. Not until desire is aroused and uneasiness excited, does the greater good determine the will. For, only through the mediation of desire, does a good object pass from a purely theoretical to a practical, appetitive relation with the mind. More precisely stated, then, the will is determined, for the most

---

[33] *Ibid.*, II, xxi, 7–57 (Fraser, I, 315–353). Cf. A Messer, "Die Behandlung des Freiheitsproblems bei John Locke," *Archiv für Geschichte der Philosophie*, 11 (1898), 133–149, 404–432, which highlights the Scholastic distinctions employed by Locke's Dutch friend, Philip van Limborch, with whom he discussed freedom.

part, by the most urgent, *present uneasiness* or particular manifestation of our general desire for happiness.

For the most part, but not always. Man is no mere plaything of the dialectic of conflicting desires: both materialistic and rationalistic determinism misread his mode of choice. Experience shows that a man can suspend his desires sufficiently, so that they do not determine his will, until he can subject their objects to due examination. This *suspension of the effective operation of desires,* in order to insure a fair inquiry into the good and evil of proposed actions, is the source of man's liberty. The very necessity of our pursuit of happiness in general permits us to be free from any absolute determination by desire for particular goods. We can suspend our pursuit of a particular good long enough to ask whether it will really contribute toward our total happiness, and effectively enough to preserve our freedom of choice. In this way, men can determine for themselves what is to be taken as a necessary, particular component of their happiness and hence as the most pressing and important uneasiness in the present situation.

To this extent, man has some freedom for morally responsible *action.* Freedom is not cultivated indifference or self-centeredness: it has an end and a use. It enables us to attain a good of our own choosing. The agent desires, wills, and acts in conformity with a deliberate appraisal of the object. A man's will is determined by his own judgment about what is worth seeking. Actions, determined ultimately by one's own mature judgment, are the mark and fruit of freedom. In this argumentation, Locke has made his own empirical adaptation of the discussions of freedom presented in the Scholastic textbooks, which his Dutch friends summarized.

Locke's deepest influence upon practical thinking was felt in *social* and *political philosophy.* In reflecting upon the political situation in the England of James II and William III, he sought to discover some general and permanent conditions of political life. As the immediate target of his criticism, he chose Sir Robert Filmer's *Patriarcha or The Natural Power of Kings* (1680). In this and other writings, Filmer had defended the theory of the divine right of kings, the paternal or patriarchal nature of royal power, and the absolute monarchy. It was against this last contention that Locke's most serious arguments were directed. He was no opponent of the monarchial form of government, but he supported the Whig Settlement, involving a constitutional rather than an absolute monarchy. It was no mere coincidence that his political theories should agree in the main with Whig policies. Locke provided the "Glorious Revolution" with an apologia and a platform, supplying the backbone of political thinking and institutions in the English-speaking countries for several generations. He gave clear and unified expression to a number of current social and political concepts, that were ripe for such a synthesis. He provided a way of using the notions of the state of nature, personal liberty, the social contract, and the rule of the majority, in the service of a constitutional monarchy.

In the *Second Treatise of Civil Government,* Locke transfers to the social plane his basic practical tension between a definitive knowledge of the *natural law* and the working criterion of *personal preservation* and happiness. He reaffirms, in a more informal and popular way, his view that the natural law is a declaration of the will of God. But this eternal rule is addressed to human agents and must be promulgated through the workings of man's own mature reason. Considered concretely and historically, however, men are often ignorant of God as the author and sanction of the natural law, so that for them this law is not formally and effectively accepted as the law of their lives. But they do respond vigorously to the actual promptings of the fundamental law of nature: the self-preservation of mankind. They recognize their natural right to life itself, to the power of appropriating goods, and to the pursuit of happiness. Although Locke is confident that human reason can ground these rights ultimately in the natural law, taken in its plenary meaning, he undertakes to construct his social and political philosophy upon the immediate conviction of the individual in his right to self-preservation.

For one thing, this tendency is common to all men, binding them together into what Locke refers to as the universal society or great natural community of mankind. As Hobbes had observed, men must live together in a common world, even before they join in civil society. The original condition is that of the *state of nature,* which Locke understands to be the condition of living together under the guidance of our natural reason, but without any settled superior power.[34] He differentiates between his own state of nature and that outlined by Hobbes, since the Hobbesian state of nature is essentially a state of war of all against all. Although Locke grants that in practice his

[34] Chapter Two of *The Second Treatise of Civil Government* is entitled: "Of the State of Nature" (Cook, 122–128).

view of the state of nature also leads to perpetual conflict, he does not define it essentially as a declared intent of applying force, without right, upon another person. The state of nature is not anarchical, since men are always endowed with the law of nature or reason. But under unsettled social conditions, men do not reflect sufficiently and hence deprive this law of its proper promulgation. Only through the consequences of trying to pursue their self-interest, can men see the need to establish and follow rules of conduct.

The state of nature is one in which men are all free and equal. Natural *freedom* is not an unbounded right to do as one pleases. The right of self-preservation assures each man of a twofold freedom: to do all in his power for the preservation of his life, liberty, and possessions, and to judge and punish those who damage him in these respects. These rights are not absolute in their exercise, however, since the individual must pursue his welfare with a view to the peace and improvement of all mankind. He should also temper his punishment of a wrongdoer by the rational intent of securing reparation and the reintroduction of the offender into the community of mankind. Similarly, the *equality* of men does not wipe out differences of age, birth, capacity, and virtue. Their basic equality resides precisely in the sphere of dominion: every man is absolute lord over himself, and no man is rightfully subject to the will or authority of another. Men in the natural state are independent of one another, as far as any rightful submission of one individual to another is concerned. Each has an equal share in freedom, the preservation and cultivation of which is the main end of the law of nature.

Yet *want* is not absent from the state of nature, since bodily needs are present, urgent, and slackless. This natural fact provides Locke's theory with the dynamism required to generate both property and the body politic. Locke appropriates the medieval commonplace that, in the beginning, God gave all material goods to men in common. But He also constituted men of such a frame that they need to consume these goods, and can do so only with the help of their own labor. A man's fundamental *propriety* or *dominion* is over his own person, activity, and labor.[35] His radical, social freedom lies in his power to dispose his own being and labor as he will, within the general framework of the natural law. Since he cannot gather or develop material goods without mixing therein something of his

[35] On property, see *ibid.,* V (Cook, 133–146); J. P. Day, "Locke on Property," *Philosophical Quarterly,* 16 (1966), 207–220.

own labor and personality, he cannot satisfy his natural wants without appropriating things to himself. The earth and its riches cannot be used in a human way, without establishing individual dominion over them. This is the foundation for the right to *private property*.

The will of God and the promptings of his own nature incline a man to labor: to use this power is, unavoidably, to appropriate goods to himself or make them his own property. Marx's labor theory of value is anticipated by Locke's remarks that, in the state of nature, property rests on *labor* (the active extension of self-dominion to embrace the things to which a man donates something of himself), and that ninety-nine hundreths of the value of goods derives from the labor expended in developing them. But labor remains, for Locke, an *individual* rather than a *social* act and, similarly, property value is created by the private individual and not by civil society. Like other natural rights, that to property must respect certain conditions placed upon its exercise. The amount of privately owned goods is limited, in the state of nature, by the individual's ability to appropriate them by his labor, as well as by his ability to consume them, without letting them spoil. This simple limitation gives way, eventually, to the complicated opportunities for acquisition permitted by the introduction of money as a medium of value and commercial exchange. Where money and commerce prevail, Locke maintains that there is a tacit social consent to the accumulation of many more times the amount of goods or value than the individual can gain by his personal labor or than he needs for personal consumption, and that he now has the right to such widened property gains. The transition from the state of nature to the settled framework of civil society means a transition from an economy of scarcity to one of plenty. Civil laws regulate the exercise of the property right, in view of the ends for which men have banded together in the political community. This social regulation of property is intended, however, to secure each man in his right to accumulate goods, since this tends to increase the general good of society.

Material possessions constitute a major, although not the sole, occasion for the passage from the state of nature to civil society. If Locke's state of nature is not amoral, it is nevertheless subject to the same *intolerable conditions* that plagued the Hobbesian state of nature. Men are prone to overreach their neighbors in search of an unreasonable amount of power, honor, and property. Appeal to the natural law is insufficient to restrain them or secure harmony. For the natural law is unwritten: its dictates remain obscure to the indolent, and tempt the passionate or selfish to pervert them in practice. The state of nature lacks three *essential elements of a stable society:* a clearly known and publicly accepted law, an impartial judge of disputes, and an adequate power to execute sentences by force, used in the service of right.[36] Instead, every man is his own judge and executioner. His judgments are apt to be passed in his own favor, whereas his ability to carry them out is often lacking. In the state of nature, then, the preservation of life, liberty, and estate is an extremely precarious undertaking. The insecurity and inconvenience of this condition impel men to unite in political society.

Locke refers to the motive behind this transition, variously, as a *voluntary inclination,* a *need,* and a *compulsion.* Apparently, the more definite arrangement of life in civil society is in accord with the promptings of human nature, as constituted by God. But Locke touches only lightly on this natural inclination and love of men for a regulated social life, since his polemical aim requires him to lay stress upon the independence and equality of men in their natural state. Man is a political animal not so much by nature as by reason of the deficiencies of his natural condition. Hence, Locke often follows Hobbes in explaining how the insecurities of natural, non-political existence "drive" men into civil society, forcing them to "take sanctuary" in government and to accept the bonds of law.[37] Several times, he makes a contrast between what is natural and what is social or political. Locke's natural man is not completely asocial, since he is organized along with others, under the natural law. But he is lacking in the main ingredient of any terrestrial society: submission to recognized public authority, having the right to legislate and the power to exact penalties.

Earthly civil society is fully constituted only with the erection of the political power, which men are driven to establish, because of the inconveniences accompanying its absence. Each independent individual agrees to forego two of his natural powers: that of doing whatsoever he sees fit (within the bounds of the law of reason or nature) to secure the preservation of himself and others, and that of

---

[36] *Ibid.,* IX, 124–126 (Cook, 184–185).

[37] *The Second Treatise of Civil Government,* IX, 127 (Cook, 185). Formal reference is made, however, to "necessity, convenience, and inclination," in *ibid.,* VII, 77 (Cook, 159), as joint motives provided by God for impelling men to join in civil society. The comparison with Hobbes is developed by H. Johnston, "Locke's Leviathan," *The Modern Schoolman,* 26 (1948–1949), 201–210.

acting as his own judge and punisher of crime. The latter power is surrendered completely to the community and replaced by public authority, whereas the former is foregone in the degree that the welfare of men is promoted by civil laws. The transfer of individual powers to the community is made through the *social contract* or compact, which rests on the freely given consent of the individuals involved.[38] Only when men agree to make this transfer and thus institute the public authority of the community, can they be said to belong to political society.

Locke construes the social contract in such fashion that neither Filmer's absolute monarchy nor Hobbes' Leviathan will result. Political power and authority reside in the people or community as a whole, and not in the person of an absolute monarch. Moreover, the effective aims of the community are determined by the will of the majority, which is directed toward the common good of the whole people. Government is established only as a definite way of carrying out the will of the majority and thus securing the common good of the community. Laws enacted by the legislature must conform with the long-range end of civil society: *the better preservation of property* — understood in the inclusive sense of the integrity of life, liberty, and possessions. Public authority will revert to the people as a whole, either at the expiration of the term of a government (if some temporal limit has been specified for it) or through forfeiture on the part of a government that misuses political power and perverts the ends of legislation. Government is by the consent of the governed and for the sake of an increase of freedom among the citizens. When life, liberty, and possessions are endangered through the use of political authority by a particular government, the existing laws are unjust and the government tyrannous. Under such circumstances, revolution against the oppressive regime is permitted, in order to reorientate the political community toward its proper goal.

Three points in this social theory have come under frequent criticism, ever since Locke's own day: the concept of the state of nature, the meaning of the common good, and the right of property.

1. Just as Locke analytically reduces the richness of cognitive experience to its two inlets and its ideal elements, so he analytically reduces the social life of men to the atomic individuals, from which it might be supposed to originate. He never makes it quite clear

---

[38] *The Second Treatise of Civil Government,* VIII, 95–99, 116–122 (Cook, 168–170, 180–183).

whether the state of nature is intended *historically* or as a rational concept and *analytical* limit. He often refers to an actual state of affairs, when "in the beginning all the world was America,"[39] and along this historical line he mentions various institutional developments and travelers' reports. But his main procedure is to prove the state of nature by rational analysis. Taking as a definition of the state of nature, the absence of any freely and rationally accepted earthly law and judge, Locke exemplifies it by the relations among heads of nations (agreeing with Hobbes' description of the "natural" condition of continuous conflict in international life), the status of children, and the master-slave relationship. He does not extend his reasoning about the inconveniences of natural existence to the inference that a world political community should be placed over the national, sovereign states. The example of children is illuminating, since on Locke's premises, they are not members of the political community, for lack of giving free, express consent. On this reasoning, it makes no difference whether one has been raised in a long-established society or brought up in the wilds: he is in the state of nature and is not a member of the civil community. Locke does allow that enjoyment of property entails a tacit consent to abide by the laws of the land. But this tacit consent is not enough to make a man a member of that civil society, since such incorporation rests on an actual and explicit agreement. In this respect, Locke is more radically individualistic than Hobbes, who maintains that tacit consent is sufficient to incorporate men into a given political community.

2. Perhaps the most elusive notion in Locke's political philosophy is that of the common good. Neither in the state of nature nor in civil society is the individual permitted to seek his own welfare at the expense of others or to their total neglect. Locke acknowledges the natural-law basis for the general welfare of mankind in almost every context where he defends the individual's concern for his own liberty and happiness. He declares that government and law are ordained to the general good of those under the law. But he never firmly establishes the meaning of a distinctive *common good of society,* which cannot be resolved simply into the *aggregate sum of individual goods* or into the *interests of the majority.* All of the social criteria proposed by Locke are affected by the powerful tendency

---

[39] *Ibid.,* V, 49 (Cook, 145). To those who objected that there is no historical evidence about men living in the state of pure nature and then coming together for a social contract in "the mighty leviathan," Locke replied that the state of nature is not conducive to the writing of history and that government antecedes written records.

of his philosophical method toward analytic reduction of the common good to that of many individuals, having natural rights. This introduces a certain ambivalence into Locke's view of the relation between the government and the public good. He speaks in traditional language of the dedication of political power and legislation to the betterment of the whole people, and yet he also refers to the state as an umpire, settling disputes among individuals. In last analysis, the state is an instrument of the people, and yet the welfare of the people is determined by the self-interests of the majority. Locke's trust in the rectitude of the will of the majority, as invariably promoting the well-being of the whole community, rests in part upon the contingent circumstances surrounding the Whig Settlement in England, and in part upon his general conviction that practical life must be regulated by readily ascertained probabilities. This theory of government counteracts any idolatry of the state, but it does not meet the need for well-determined safeguards against a tyrannous majority, with whom the political power ultimately lies. This problem became acute by the time of John Stuart Mill, in the nineteenth century, and is even more urgent in our day, due to the threats and fascinations of totalitarianism.

3. Locke's ambiguous treatment of the common good benefited the growing *capitalist* conception of property. The majority he had in mind were the leaders in commerce and banking, who were coming to wield effective social power. Despite his generous conception of "property," as including the happiness and liberty of individuals, Locke's dictum that "government has no other end but the preservation of property,"[40] worked historically as a bulwark of individualistic and laissez-faire policies. Locke wanted to regulate the accumulation of property by the requirements of the community as a whole, but the common good in turn resolved itself into the search of the majority of individuals for their own prosperity. Hence, in practice, the "preservation" of property meant the provision of stable conditions for a dynamic increase in the rate of individual accumulation.

Locke did not succeed in reintegrating the impulse toward self-preservation with the natural law, as a declaration of God's will. This was reflected in his shift from *duties* to *rights,* which are extensions of the individual's urge toward self-preservation.[41] Locke's moral volun-

---

[40] *Ibid.,* VII, 94 (Cook, 168); cf. VII, 87 (Cook, 163), on government acting as an umpire.

[41] Read L. Strauss' penetrating study, "On Locke's Doctrine of Natural Right," *The Philosophical Review,* 51 (1952), 475–502.

tarism encouraged the emphasis upon rights, regarded as moral powers resident in persons. This subjective view of rights was not integrated firmly with any objective foundation of rights in the relations among persons and their joint relation with the common good. Hence the property right was not grounded in a relation of objective justice among men and between men and the community, in respect to external goods. With this definite measure and control of the personal disposition of property eliminated, it was easy for proponents of economic individualism to dispense entirely with the common good or social purpose, as a relevant standard for regulating the use of property.

SUMMARY

Locke observed that we cannot undertake high metaphysical investigations without first discovering the capacity and limits of the human understanding. He approached this latter task with the aid of the historical plain method, which studies the mind in its actual operation, apart from physiological and metaphysical inquiries about the whence and whither of cognition. But the understanding cannot be divorced from ideas, which are the objects about which it is concerned. After eliminating innate principles and ideas, Locke was left with the mind as a clean tablet, and with experience as the only certified stylus. Taking sensation and reflection as the twin sources of experience, he set about classifying ideas according to the mental powers and operations by which they are received and then correlated. He made a vigorous case for the classical modern doctrine on the subjectivity of what men usually regard as real, secondary qualities, but he did not elucidate how the ideas of primary qualities can be both other than, and similar to, the primary qualities themselves. The Lockean way of ideas yielded a psychological explanation of efficient causality and human personality, although it did not open up any road to a philosophical knowledge of the real essence of substances, spiritual or material. Locke proposed a doctrine of abstraction based upon the mental operations of separating and relating. General meaning is due to the mind's ability to relate an idea to several particulars, which it is then able to represent. Since Locke defined knowledge as a perception of agreement or disagreement among ideas, he felt confident about specifying beforehand the limits of strict knowledge. He distinguished between intuitive knowledge of oneself, demonstrative knowledge of God, and sensitive knowledge of the external world. Although intuition and demonstration are the supreme modes of general knowledge, Locke sought to locate sense knowledge of the world a little below genuine demonstration and yet a little above probability. In practical philosophy, he defended man's freedom, proposed a doctrine on the state of nature and the subjective right to property, and gave a version of the social contract permitting constitutional control of the ruler by the people.

BIBLIOGRAPHICAL NOTE

1. *Sources.* There is in preparation a long awaited, critical collected edition of Locke, to be published by Oxford University Press, beginning with the correspondence. Two older collections are: *The Works of John Locke* (tenth ed., 10 Vols., London, Johnson, 1801); J. A. St. John, ed., *The Philosophical Works of John Locke* (2 Vols., London, Bohn, 1854), containing: *On the Conduct of the Understanding, An Essay concerning Human Understanding, Controversy with Bishop Stillingfleet, An Examination of P. Malebranche's Opinion, Elements of Natural Philosophy,* and *Some Thoughts concerning Reading.* There are two convenient editions of the *Essay: An Essay concerning Human Understanding,* ed. by A. C. Fraser (reprint, 2 Vols., New York: Dover, 1959), with annotations that must be used with caution; *An Essay concerning Human Understanding,* ed. by J. W. Yolton (2 Vols., New York: Dutton, 1961). The Lovelace Collection of Locke's papers is a rich trove, from which the following books have been derived: *An Essay concerning the Understanding, Knowledge, Opinion and Assent* (Cambridge: Harvard University Press, 1931), ed. by B. Rand; *An Early Draft of Locke's Essay, together with Excerpts from His Journals* (Oxford: Clarendon, 1936), ed. by R. I. Aaron and J. Gibb; *Locke's Travels in France, 1675–1679* (Cambridge: the University Press, 1953), ed. by J. Lough; *Essays on the Law of Nature* (Oxford: Clarendon, 1954), ed. by W. von Leyden. The Aaron-Gibb text of the early version of the *Essay* is earlier and better edited than the Rand text; the travel book gives valuable examples of Locke's descriptive method. *Two Tracts on Government,* ed. by P. Abrams (Cambridge: The University Press, 1967) is an early (1660) authoritarian view.

There is a critical edition of Locke's *Two Treatises of Government* (Cambridge: the University Press, 1960); (reprint, New York: New American Library Mentor Books, 1965), ed. by P. Laslett, who contributes an informative introduction. The full text of Sir Robert Filmer's famous *Patriarcha,* with which Locke was preoccupied, is given in T. I. Cook's ed. of Locke's *Two Treatises of Government* (New York: Hafner, 1947); and H. R. Penniman's ed. of John Locke, *On Politics and Education* (New York: Van Nostrand, 1947), contains *Some Thoughts concerning Education.* The Latin and English texts of Locke's *A Letter concerning Toleration* (The Hague: Nijhoff, 1963), ed. by M. Montuori, establishes the treatise-character of the first *Letter.* Locke's *The Reasonableness of Christianity* (Stanford: Stanford University Press, 1958), is abridged and edited with an acute Introduction by I. T. Ramsey, who adds Locke's *A Discourse of Miracles* and part of *A Third Letter concerning Toleration.* Different facets of Locke's mind can be appreciated through two collections of his letters: H. Ollion and T. J. De Boer, eds., *Lettres inédites de John Locke* (The Hague: Nijhoff, 1912), reflecting his interest in theological issues of free will raised by his Dutch theologian friends; B. Rand, ed., *The Correspondence of John Locke and Edward Clarke* (Cambridge: Harvard University Press, 1927), shows Locke as a family friend, economist, and student of political affairs.

2. *Studies.* The newly opened Lovelace sources are the basis for Maurice Cranston's fine biography, *John Locke* (New York: Macmillan, 1957). Two older biographies are still worth consulting: Lord King's *The Life of John Locke* (new ed., 2 Vols., London: Colburn and Bentley, 1830), and the derivative work by H. R. Fox Bourne, *The Life of John Locke* (2 Vols., New York: Harper, 1876). The impact of Locke's medical training upon his thought is stressed in Kenneth Dewhurst, *John Locke, 1632-1704, Physician and Philosopher* (London: Wellcome Historical Medical Library, 1963). Further insight is gained from studies of his library and readings: J. Harrison and P. Laslett, eds., *The Library of John Locke* (Oxford: Oxford University Press, 1965); G. Bonno, *Les Relations intellectuelles de Locke avec la France* (Berkeley: University of California Press, 1955). Three general introductions to his philosophy are noteworthy: R. I. Aaron, *John Locke* (second ed., New York: Oxford University Press, 1955); D. J. O'Connor, *John Locke* (Baltimore: Penguin Books, 1952); C. A. Viano, *John Locke, Dal razionalismo all' illuminismo* (Turin, Einaudi, 1960). Aaron is historically oriented; O'Connor makes an analytic restatement; and Viano reverses the usual order by working from Locke's political, social, religious, and scientific interests to his theory of knowledge.

Locke's epistemology and theoretical philosophy are examined by: J. Gibson, *Locke's Theory of Knowledge and Its Historical Relations* (Cambridge: the University Press, 1917), with historical comparisons somewhat flawed by insufficient data; J. G. Clapp, *Locke's Conception of the Mind* (privately published Columbia University dissertation, 1937), on mind as power, substance, and knower; A. Klemmt, *John Locke: Theoretische Philosophie* (Meisenheim: Hain, 1952), a careful analytic account. Despite the work of É. Krakowski, *Les Sources médiévales de la philosophie de Locke* (Paris: Jouve, 1915), and A. Tellkamp, *Das Verhältnis John Lockes zur Scholastik* (Münster: Aschendorff, 1927), Locke's precise relationship with current scholastic and university philosophy is still to be determined from the sources. On his moral and political philosophy, see: A. Petzäll, *Ethics and Epistemology in John Locke's Essay concerning Human Understanding* (Göteborg: Wettergren and Kerber, 1937); S. P. Lamprecht, *The Moral and Political Philosophy of John Locke* (New York: Columbia University Press, 1918); C. J. Cjaikowski, *The Theory of Private Property in John Locke's Political Philosophy* (privately published University of Notre Dame dissertation, 1941); J. W. Gough, *Locke's Political Philosophy* (New York: Oxford University Press, 1950), making debatable use of the private papers; R. H. Cox, *Locke on War and Peace* (New York: Oxford University Press, 1960); R. Polin, *La Politique morale de John Locke* (Paris: Presses Universitaires, 1960), perhaps the most balanced presentation. Locke's religious position and impact on religious thought are studied by: S. G. Hefelbower, *The Relation of John Locke to English Deism* (Chicago: University of Chicago Press, 1918); J. W. Yolton, *John Locke and the Way of Ideas* (New York: Oxford University Press, 1956), which traces the religious controversies he aroused; H. G. Van Leewen, *The Problem of Certainty in English Thought, 1630-*

1690 (The Hague: Nijhoff, 1963), depicting Locke as the climax of an effort to overcome skepticism with a theory of degrees of certainty.

3. *British Empiricism and Cambridge Platonism.* Locke's social and cultural milieu can be grasped from G. N. Clark, *The Seventeenth Century* (second ed. New York: Oxford University Press Galaxy Book, 1961), and Basil Willey, *The Seventeenth-Century Background* (New York: Doubleday Anchor Book, 1953). B. Willey's *The Eighteenth-Century Background* (Boston: Beacon Press, 1961) shows how Locke and Newton dominated the following century's discussion of "nature." M. H. Carré, *Phases of Thought in England* (Oxford: Clarendon, 1949), interweaves philosophy with the theological, literary, and scientific interests in England, whereas W. R. Sorley's *A History of British Philosophy to 1900,* (reprint, Cambridge: the University Press, 1965) follows the internal development of philosophy itself. On classical British empiricism, consult: C. R. Morris, *Locke, Berkeley, Hume* (Oxford: Clarendon, 1931); R. Reininger, *Locke, Berkeley, Hume* (Munich: Reinhardt, 1922); E. Leroux and A.-L. Leroy, *La Philosophie anglaise classique* (Paris: Colin, 1951). Readings include: E. A. Burtt, ed., *The English Philosophers from Bacon to Mill* (New York: Modern Library, 1939); A. Ayer and R. Winch, eds., *British Empirical Philosophy* (London: Routledge and Kegan Paul, 1952). M. H. Mandelbaum, *Philosophy, Science, and Sense Perception* (Baltimore: Johns Hopkins Press, 1964), examines Locke and Hume from the standpoint of a realism critically responsive to the scientific relationship with the world.

As a counter-theme to the usual emphasis placed on the empiricist strain in British thought, the idealistic current becomes central in J. H. Muirhead's *The Platonic Tradition in Anglo-Saxon Philosophy* (New York: Humanities Press, 1965), with Cambridge Platonism constituting the first phase. The philosophic side of Cambridge Platonism is analyzed by E. Cassirer, *The Platonic Renaissance in England* (Austin: University of Texas Press, 1953), and its religious aspects are examined in two well informed studies: G. P. Pawson, *The Cambridge Platonists and Their Place in Religious Thought* (London: SPCK Press, 1930), and W. C. de Pauley, *The Candle of the Lord: Studies in the Cambridge Platonists* (New York: Macmillan, 1937). The two leaders of this school are the subjects of separate monographs: J. A. Passmore, *Ralph Cudworth: An Interpretation* (Cambridge: the University Press, 1951), and A. Liechtenstein, *Henry More* (Cambridge: Harvard University Press, 1962). Source readings are furnished in E. T. Compagnac's *The Cambridge Platonists* (Oxford: Clarendon, 1901).

Chapter II. GEORGE BERKELEY

I. LIFE AND WRITINGS

GEORGE BERKELEY, an Irishman of English ancestry, was born in Kilkenny in 1685. He matriculated at Trinity College, Dublin, in 1700, receiving the degrees of bachelor and master of arts and, later on, bachelor and doctor of divinity. Appointed a fellow of Trinity in 1707, he served as tutor and lecturer there for two periods: 1707–1713 and 1721–1724. During the first period of service, his philosophical genius matured rapidly and his basic works were written. At Trinity, Locke and Descartes were staple fare, while considerable attention was also paid to Malebranche, Newton, and Clarke. The views of Hobbes and later freethinkers were critically discussed, but Berkeley was soon convinced that the issues could not be settled as long as both sides accepted the reality of matter. His first approach to the immaterialist hypothesis was made in two notebooks, written in 1707–1708, the so-called *Philosophical Commentaries* (discovered and published in a defective edition, 1871; accurate edition, 1944). Berkeley ventured to publish part of his findings, bearing on the sense of sight, in *An Essay Towards a New Theory of Vision* (1709). There, he established the mental nature of the actual object of sight, although he accorded extramental reality to the object of touch. His thorough-going immaterialism was explained and defended in *A Treatise concerning the Principles of Human Knowledge* (1710). Since some of his friends regarded the theory as oversubtle and mad, Berkeley recast his thought in popular form and stressed its accord with common sense, in *Three Dialogues between Hylas and Philonous* (1713). Thus, before his thirtieth year, Berkeley had set forth his entire system of philosophy and carefully weighed the objections commonly raised against it.

In order to broaden his experience, he went to London in 1713 and became the companion of such wits as Swift, Steele, Addison,

Gay, Pope, Prior, and Arbuthnot. A series of anonymous articles against freethinking was contributed by Berkeley to Steele's *Guardian*. He was a member of the party accompanying Lord Peterborough to the coronation of the King of Sicily and, during this trip (1713–1714), he may have had a philosophical interview with Malebranche. There followed a four-year tour of France and Italy (1716–1720), during which Berkeley acted as tutor to a friend's son, began a treatise on psychology and ethics (lost in an accident), and wrote a short work *On Motion* (1721), in which the relations between immaterialism and the mechanical sciences were discussed. After his return to London, Berkeley was impressed by the corruption and frivolity of society, as exemplified by the panic upon the bursting of the South Sea Bubble, a fabulous financial scheme. He resumed his lecturing at Trinity College but was convinced (as the famous line from his own poem reads) that "westward the course of empire takes its way." Berkeley resigned his Trinity fellowship upon being appointed Dean of Derry (1724). He then made elaborate plans for the founding of St. Paul's College in Bermuda, having as its purpose the education of sons of English planters and native Indians both for the ministry and for useful work in agriculture and trade. A charter was obtained in 1725, some subscription monies were raised, and both the King and Parliament agreed to a grant of 20,000 pounds. On the strength of this assurance, Berkeley took his newly wedded wife to Newport, Rhode Island, in 1729 and built a house called Whitehall. (The edifice is still in good condition.) He wanted to develop the Newport farm into a continental base for his proposed college and also to survey the American situation at firsthand. While in America, he corresponded with the American idealistic philosopher, Samuel Johnson, and wrote a sustained critique of freethinking: *Alciphron or the Minute Philosopher* (1732). The British prime minister, Robert Walpole, was finally persuaded not to pay the grant to the college, so that in 1731 the disappointed Berkeley returned to England. As a parting gift to America, he left his books to Yale and Harvard libraries and deeded his house and estate at Newport to Yale University for the support of three scholars.

As recognition of his faithful service in the Church of Ireland, Berkeley was appointed Bishop of Cloyne (1734). He labored for twenty years for the spiritual and material welfare of his flock, instituting economic self-help programs and offering his famous remedy of tar water as a cure for dysentery and other diseases afflicting the people. His last important work was *Siris, a Chain of Philosophical Reflexions and Inquiries Concerning the Virtues of Tar-Water* (1744), which (as Coleridge put it) begins with tar water and ends with the Holy Trinity, the *omne scibile* forming the interspace. In 1752, Berkeley went to Oxford to see his son, George, safely settled in his studies. He died peacefully in January of the following year, while his wife was reading the passage in St. Paul's first letter to the Corinthians on Christ's victory over death.

2. ABSTRACTION AND THE SENSIBLE THING

From his study of Descartes and Malebranche, Locke and Newton, Berkeley familiarized himself thoroughly with the main trends in seventeenth-century philosophy. His own position grew out of an attempt to describe experience from the accepted starting point in the mind, having its own ideas as its direct objects. The main question raised by his predecessors concerned how the human mind can bridge the chasm between its own ideas and the surrounding world, so that we can have some objective certainty about real things. The answers given to this question were quite divergent and not very convincing to Berkeley, who viewed them in the light of the rising tide of popular, eighteenth-century skepticism. The skeptical currents of thought would not be so strong, he reasoned, if there were not a fundamental weakness about all the previous constructive answers. Berkeley did not challenge the accepted *mentalistic starting point* of philosophical inquiry. But he did bring criticism to bear upon the way in which the main philosophical *question* itself had been posed. For, to ask how a passage can be made from mind to things, is to suppose that sensible things are really different from our ideas or mental objects. Berkeley's entire philosophical effort stems from a removal of this supposition. He reformulated the major philosophical problem, to read: how can a coherent account of the world be given, if the idea or mental object and the real sensible thing are one and the same? If a successful explanation of sensible reality can be furnished, under this condition, then the skeptics will forever be quieted. For, there will be no further need to search behind our ideas for another world, to which our ideas must be shown to conform. The perilous uncertainty of such an influence is to be removed by the radical expedient of denying the need and the meaningfulness of a hidden order of sensible entities.

Berkeley stated this fresh hypothesis in what he termed his New

Principle. In one of his early philosophical commentaries, he gave a succinct and comprehensive formulation of the *New Principle*: "Existence is *percipi* or *percipere* or *velle*, i.e., *agere.*"[1] This statement shows that, for Berkeley, the crucial issue in philosophy concerns the meaning of existence. His answer was that "existence" has two distinct and even opposed meanings. It signifies either the state of being perceived or the act of perceiving, which is basically the same as willing and acting. *To-be-perceived* is the kind of existence belonging to the *sensible thing:* its entire to-be consists in its to-be-perceived. Hence there is no real distinction between the real sensible thing and the mental object, called the idea of the sensible thing. But there is a real distinction between the sensible existent or mental object and the perceiver. *To perceive* is the sort of existence proper to the *mind:* its to-be is that of an active, perceiving, and willing principle. Hence sensible things and minds are the sole existents — and sensible things are identical with the ideas of sense possessed by minds.

In order to clear the path for acceptance of his New Principle, Berkeley had to perform a negative and a positive task. (1) The negative step was taken in his *critique of abstraction.* This move was dictated by the obvious retort that any Lockean thinker would give to Berkeley's theory of sensible existence. The Lockean reply would be a distinction between the thing's mental presence and its real existence, as a movable, extended substance, outside the mind. Since the force of this distinction depends upon our ability to abstract sensible existence, motion, and extension from the condition of being perceived, Berkeley was obliged to criticize Locke's theory of abstraction and abstract, general ideas. (2) The positive move was to offer a new *definition of the sensible thing,* in line with the requirements of the New Principle. Since Berkeley agreed with Descartes and Locke that the idea is the formal and direct object of the mind, his strategy was to show that a starting point in ideas must lead to such a definition of the sensible thing as would confirm his theory of sensible existence. Once these two steps were taken, there was nothing to prevent Berkeley from indicating the metaphysical consequences of his New Principle. It issues in an *empirical immaterialism,* in which material substance is eliminated and the totality of experience is explained in function of the infinite mind, finite minds, ideas, and notions.

---

[1] *Philosophical Commentaries*, 429–429a. All references in Berkeley are to the Luce-Jessop edition of *The Works of George Berkeley, Bishop of Cloyne;* cf. I, 53 (italics and punctuation added). This edition is referred to hereafter as *Works.*

1. *The Critique of Abstraction.* Although Berkeley decries the learned dust raised by "the Schoolmen, those great masters of abstraction,"[2] his real target of criticism is Locke. As representative of what is commonly meant by an abstract, general idea, he quotes the passage (see above, p. 30) in which Locke describes the idea of a triangle. Berkeley gives practically a word-for-word commentary on this text, which was so familiar to his contemporaries.

First, he bids us notice how Locke stresses the *difficulty* of forming these abstract ideas. It follows that abstraction is not an easy process, one to be performed unthinkingly by children. But does there *ever* come a time, even in our mature years, when we deliberately set about to frame these ideas? And even if we should decide to do so, can we *actually form* such an idea as Locke's triangle? As a good empiricist, Berkeley invites us to try to picture to ourselves the general idea of a triangle that is "neither equilateral, equicrural, nor scalenon; but all and none of these at once." He challenges us to try to visualize the general, abstract idea of color, which is neither white nor black, nor any other particular shade, but something abstracted from all of these. Little wonder that Locke should confess that the abstract, general idea contains inconsistent elements. For his own part, Berkeley reports that he always has in mind some particular shape or color, and never entertains a bare, abstract idea of shape as such or color as such.

Berkeley was unable, however, to press this psychological argument very far. For it rested on the assumption that an idea is only a percept or image, and that abstraction is a process of picturing or *concrete visualization* of the object. If this assumption is admitted, it is obvious that some concrete image must always be kept in mind. But the Cartesians would reply that, at the philosophical level of clear and distinct ideas, abstraction is an act of purely intellectual apprehension, which cannot be confined to the conditions of sense imagery. Furthermore, the psychological argument may prove too much, if it implies a denial of universal meaning. For then, philosophical inference is rendered impossible, and even a system of empirical immaterialism is ruled out.

These considerations forced Berkeley to introduce a capital dis-

---

[2] *The Principles of Human Knowledge*, Introduction, 17 (*Works*, II, 35). This Introduction to the *Principles* (*Works*, II, 25–40) is the *locus classicus* for Berkeley's attack on abstraction. See also *An Essay towards a New Theory of Vision*, 122–131 (*Works*, I, 220–224).

tinction between the *abstractness* and the *generality* of ideas. He sought a way to reject the former trait and yet retain the latter. The abstract character of ideas is founded on two pretended operations of the mind: (*a*) the claim to be able to frame an "absolute, positive nature or conception of any thing,"[3] such as the idea of motion as such, apart from any particular kind of motion, and yet corresponding to them all; (*b*) the claim to be able to separate mentally those traits or qualities that cannot possibly exist separately, such as the idea of motion as such, apart from the body that moves. These two operations constitute what Berkeley termed *abstraction proper*. He remained unalterably opposed to abstraction proper and to the abstract ideas, which are its supposed outcome. For, each of these abstracting operations would provide an entering wedge against the validity of his New Principle. Thus, the Cartesians would separate extension and motion as such from their particular modes, and would then give a clear and distinct definition of material substance and thereby prove its extramental reality. And the Lockeans would separate sensible existence as such from the conditions of perception, and would then attribute it to the extramental material substance. Both of these procedures illustrate what Berkeley regarded as a vicious sort of abstraction, since they disintegrate the concrete unity of the sensible existent. (*a*) If the New Principle holds good, then to grasp the absolute nature of an isolated quality as an object of perception is equivalent to attributing to it a real, sensible existence. The real existence of motion or extension, as general natures, is in violation of the commonly accepted principle that only the concrete individual can exist. (*b*) According to the New Principle, it is impossible to separate or abstract the *esse* from the *percipi* of a sensible thing. Hence it is only verbally possible to treat of a sensible existent independently of the condition of its being perceived by the mind. Berkeley regarded abstraction proper as a psychological impossibility, only because it is basically a metaphysical and epistemological impossibility, granted the truth of his New Principle.

Nevertheless, he agreed with Locke that generality of meaning is required for scientific knowledge and demonstration. Having eliminated the abstractness of our ideas, he now attempted to defend their general signification. Of the two operations invoked by Locke in

---

[3] *The Principles of Human Knowledge*, Introduction, 15 (*Works*, II, 33–34); the Scholastic manuals familiar to Locke sometimes called this the direct universal. On the two distinctive acts of abstraction proper, cf. *ibid.*, 7–10 (*Works*, II, 27–30).

explanation of general ideas — separating and relating — Berkeley rejected the first, insofar as it is a process of abstraction proper. Still, he admitted a legitimate kind of *mental separating* or *considering,* "as when I consider some particular parts or qualities separated from others, with which though they are united in some object, yet, it is possible they may really exist without them."[4] Thus the eye or the nose can be considered apart from the rest of the human body, since they may also exist in some other animal. Berkeley was quite willing to call this sort of separating or considering an abstraction, but in an *improper* sense. It never terminates in *abstract, general ideas* but only in *nonabstract, general ideas.* He made this concession, since it did not involve the crucial separation of an absolute nature from particular things, or of sensible existence from the condition of being perceived.

In further explanation of the general significance of ideas, Berkeley developed Locke's doctrine on the relating of particular ideas. Berkeley called this process a *considering* by the mind. Although the mind can never frame an abstract idea of an absolute nature, it does have the power to confine its attention to only certain aspects of the concrete, particular idea. In thinking about an isosceles triangle, for instance, the mind can focus its consideration upon this figure, precisely so far forth as it is triangular, without paying special attention to the equality of the angles or sides. The idea remains particular in its own formal nature, but it becomes *general in its signification,* since it indifferently connotes other particulars of the same sort. It can now be taken as a sign for all other particular triangular figures, toward which it stands in the functional relation of representative sign to represented objects. Similarly, although the mind never attains the abstract, general idea of man, as an absolute nature, it can consider Peter precisely insofar as he is a man. Although his particular traits are not evacuated, attention is directed toward those aspects in him which hold equally true of any other particular men. The universality of meaning does not reside in an abstracted common nature but in the function of considering certain particular traits as a sign, applicable to several other individual objects.

Berkeley's explanation of general ideas modifies Locke, in two important respects. First, he bypasses the abstract, common nature, so

---

[4] *Ibid.,* Introduction, 10 (*Works,* II, 29–30). For Berkeley's behind-the-scenes development of the distinction between abstraction and considering, cf. *Philosophical Commentaries,* 254, 318, 440 (*Works,* I, 32, 39, 54).

that there is generality of meaning, without abstractness of an ideal nature. Locke had already remarked that the abstract, general idea is imperfect and cannot exist. But Berkeley's New Principle now assures him that the inability of this presumed absolute nature to *exist* is sure proof that it cannot be *perceived* at all by the mind, since to exist and to be perceived are correlative in the sensible order. Locke was led astray by the peculiarities of *language* into supposing that an abstract general, mental entity corresponds to an abstract, general name. It is only in a verbal way that one can infer the existence of abstract, general ideas, because there are abstract, general names. Berkeley holds that words stand for particular operations, attitudes, and ideas of the mind, rather than for abstract, general ideas. In the second place, Berkeley amends the nature of the real particular things, to which any general idea is related by signification. The other particular ideas to which a general idea relates, are themselves the sensible existents, and bear *no further reference* beyond themselves, as far as sensible things are concerned. Such a reference is impossible to think about, and hence impossible to reach through abstraction, since the only to-be proper to sensible things is their to-be-perceived. On both these counts, Berkeley's corrections are dependent upon the validity of the New Principle itself.

Even after this emendation of Locke, however, Berkeley does not escape from his predecessor's basic difficulties. Lockean abstraction is not a realistic process, since it involves a manipulation of ideas, rather than a penetration of the intelligible structure of the real. Berkeley's remedy is to identify the percept with the sensible existent. He formally raises the question of how we can know that a meaning holds true for several particular ideas, considered now as particular sensible existents. His answer, however, consists in a repetition of his description of the operations of considering and signifying, whereas the question requires an explanation of *how and why* these operations can validly be performed. How can the mind determine which other particulars are, in fact, "ideas of the same sort," so that it can be sure that a certain set of traits "indifferently denotes . . . [and] holds equally true of them all"?[5] To reply that the mind attends only to those features which can be found in all other particular men, triangles, or motions, merely restates the question of how we know that other particulars can be signified together, as being human, triangular,

---

[5] *The Principles of Human Knowledge,* Introduction, 11, 12 (*Works,* II, 31, 32).

or mobile. On what grounds is the mind justified in attending to a certain group of traits and in making no mention of others? What guides the operation of considering, so that it views Peter precisely so far forth as he is a man, and carefully distinguishes these factors from the ones peculiar to himself?

The latter questions must remain unanswered in the Berkeleyan system, since a definite answer would involve a *dilemma*. Either Locke's absolute nature must be reinstated (with the consequence, for Berkeley, that this object of perception also has sensible existence) or else the barrier of mentalism must be broken through, and the admission made that the mind grasps certain similar traits in the essential natures of things, whose mode of real existence is distinct from the intentional being of the idea (with a resultant undermining of the New Principle). Since neither alternative is acceptable to Berkeley, he prefers simply to point to the fact of general meaning, without trying to supply the adequate metaphysical and epistemological bases for the fact. His removal of Lockean abstraction still leaves the problem of the relation between general meanings and particular existents fundamentally unresolved.

2. *The Definition of the Sensible Thing*. Underlying the entire discussion of abstraction is a definite theory about the sensible thing. Berkeley appeals both to common sense and to Locke's premises, in order to establish a doctrine on the nature of the sensible thing which will be in conformity with his New Principle. He asks himself, first, what is ordinarily meant by saying that there is a sound or an odor, that my desk exists, or that my horse is in the barn.[6] To assert the existence of these objects is the same as to assert that they are *perceived by some mind* — and nothing more. The common-sense meaning of sensible existence is that the sound is being heard, the odor smelled, the desk perhaps seen and felt, the horse perceived in some similar way. At the very minimum, the affirmation of the real existence of a body or sensible thing involves either recalling a past sense perception or stipulating that, if I were to place myself in the proper circumstances, I would receive the specified perceptual experience. Thus, if I were to walk out to the stable, I would see the horse to be there.

---

[6] For this interrogation of common sense, see *ibid.*, I, 3–4, 23 (*Works*, II, 42, 50–51); *Three Dialogues between Hylas and Philonous*, I (*Works*, II, 195; on the tulip one "really" sees). H. M. Bracken, "Berkeley's Realisms," *The Philosophical Quarterly*, 8 (1958), 41–53, brings out the difficulties in a common-sense realist interpretation of Berkeley, if his ideas of sense are regarded as mental sensa and not as physical objects.

And even when I am not actually perceiving the horse's existence, it is the object of actual perception perhaps for other finite minds and certainly for the infinite mind of God. No more is meant by affirming the existence of bodies or bodily qualities than their being perceived or their capacity for being perceived by the finite mind, together with their always being perceived by the divine mind.

On Locke's premises, an idea is the immediate object of thought, that about which I am thinking. But, Berkeley asks, is there any difference between the common-sense conviction that the mind is immediately concerned with the sensible thing and the Lockean doctrine that the mind is directed immediately toward the idea or mental object? That in which the cognitive operation immediately terminates is the *idea* or *sensible thing,* which are one and the same.

The Lockean mind will admit the following definition: "*Sensible things are those only which are immediately perceived by sense. . . .* Sensible things therefore are nothing else but so many sensible qualities, or combinations of sensible qualities."[7] But the same mind will balk at the inference that, since what is being immediately perceived is nothing other than an idea, therefore the entire reality of the sensible thing consists in its being perceived by the mind. The follower of Locke will interject that sensible things enjoy "a real absolute being, distinct from, and without any relation to their being perceived." Berkeley's reply is that such an existence would be quite irrelevant to what has been defined as the sensible thing, since an absolute existence would be divorced from the condition of being immediately perceived by the mind. Furthermore, an absolute or mind-independent existence could never be known by our mind, which has ideas as its immediate objects. For, "*an idea can be like nothing but an idea.*"[8] Hence if the immediately known object refers to anything else, the latter must also be of an ideal nature. The only significant distinction between idea and ideatum is one that lies wholly within the sphere of mental objects. Berkeley does allow a difference between *ideas of sense* and *ideas of imagination.* The former are immediate, irreducible presentations, simply given to the mind, whereas the latter are copies and involve a mental operation. Berkeley identifies his ideas of sense with Locke's real things or archetypes of the reality of existential knowledge. Hence

---

[7] *Three Dialogues between Hylas and Philonous,* I (*Works,* II, 175); the next quotation is from the same page.

[8] *The Principles of Human Knowledge,* I, 8 (*Works,* II, 44; italics added). See P. D. Cummins, "Berkeley's Likeness Principle," *Journal of the History of Philosophy,* 4 (1966), 63–69.

he interprets the distinction between real things and ideas to mean nothing more than the distinction between ideas of sense and those of imagination. Although the latter may be said to reflect the former, both terms in the representative relation are located squarely within the realm of ideas or mental objects. Hence the existence of sensible things is not "absolute" but is the same as their state of being perceived by the mind.

Berkeley's favorite way of defending his New Principle consists in a description of the situation of the perceiving subject. Seated at my desk, I may look out the window and see the houses, the trees, the river, and the mountains. I cannot mention these things at all, except by bringing them into the relation of objects of perception for my mind. It is impossible for me to "conceive them existing unconceived or unthought of, which is a manifest repugnancy. . . . What is conceived, is surely in the mind."[9] When we try to consider the trees by themselves, apart from any perceiving mind, we are simply forgetting or methodically refraining from mentioning the fact that they are still objects of perception for our mind and hence have only the existence of being perceived.

In America, the strongest challenge of this analysis came from R. B. Perry, following some suggestions made by his master, William James.[10] James had observed that there is a considerable difference between saying that we cannot think of a thing without actually thinking *of* it, and saying that we cannot think of a thing without thinking it *to be* an idea or mode of thought. Berkeley's description of the cognitive situation emphasizes the former statement, which is a truism, but it adduces nothing to show that every object *of* perception is nothing but an object *in* perception. As an extension of this criticism, Perry taxed Berkeley with two fallacies: that of definition by initial predication and that of the egocentric predicament. The fallacy of *definition by initial predication* consists in defining a thing's essential nature exclusively in terms of some early or familiar trait, which it displays to us. The reference of a thing to our perception shows only that it is a perceivable nature, not that its intrinsic reality consists solely in being actually perceived or having a reference to

---

[9] *The Principles of Human Knowledge*, I, 23 (Works, II, 50).

[10] R. B. Perry, *Present Philosophical Tendencies* (New York, Longmans, 1912), 126–132. James and Perry continued the criticism of the Scottish philosopher, Thomas Reid, that we can distinguish between the sensation or feeling itself and the qualitative nature which we know; cf. S. C. Rome, "The Scottish Refutation of Berkeley's Immaterialism," *Philosophy and Phenomenological Research*, 3 (1943), 313–325.

the perceiver's mind. Merely to ascertain that a thing bears a relation to consciousness is to show the intelligibility of its nature: it does not show that this nature has no other existential act than that of being actually perceived by and in consciousness. Berkeley has failed to complete the analysis of the cognitive relation. If it can be shown that this relation is an extrinsic or nonmutual one, then the fact that the thing is logically related to the mind does not determine the intrinsic nature and natural mode of existing, proper to the thing. The fallacy of the *egocentric predicament* means an attempt to infer more than is warranted from the fact that, in thinking about something, we cannot avoid referring it to our own mind. It is redundant to state that, in order to know a thing, one must know it, i.e., one must bring it into cognitive relation with one's perception. This is an inescapable condition of knowledge, regardless of the nature of the thing to be known. From this condition, nothing can be inferred about the nature of the thing, which is brought into relation with the mind. Whether that thing has a distinct physical existence of its own or has no other existence than that of being perceived, the condition remains the same and remains equally incapable of settling the issue. No metaphysical conclusion whatever can be reached by restating the common requirement of all cognition, since this requirement remains the same, no matter what the nature of the thing to be known.

Two related difficulties in Berkeley's argument are significant for realists. The first concerns his axiom that ideas can only be like other ideas. This is another truism, if the idea is taken only in its own physical being, as a mental mode. As such, it has its similitudes in other mental modes or objects in the mind. But if the idea is considered in its signifying function, it is begging the question to state that it can represent nothing else than other ideas. The point at issue concerns precisely whether the *intentional* or *signifying relation* of a concept reaches beyond its own physical condition, as a mental mode of being. Berkeley's negative answer rests on the dual assumption that the mode of being of the sign must be the same as that of the thing signified, and that an idea is always an instrumental sign.[11] Once the distinction between the intentional and physical modes of being is drawn, however, a concept can be shown to be the *intentional*

---

[11] *Three Dialogues between Hylas and Philonous,* I (*Works,* II, 203–206). For a realistic criticism, cf. J. Wild, "Berkeley's Theories of Perception," *Revue Internationale de Philosophie,* 7 (1953), 134–151. Wild overemphasizes, however, the later preoccupation of Berkeley with objectivity and rationality, since such a preoccupation is evident even in the *Philosophical Commentaries.*

likeness and *formal* sign of a thing, whose real, *physical* act of existing is distinct from the condition of being perceived. But this distinction would also tell against the New Principle, which is relevant only for the physical being of the concept or object-in-cognition, not for the act of existing of the thing that is cognized. The second point of interest concerns the manner in which Berkeley describes an "absolute" or extramental manner of existing. He specifies that it must be not only distinct from, but also entirely unrelated and unrelatable to, the mind. Yet defense of the real distinction between the physical *esse* of the existing thing and its *percipi* does not entail a denial of any possible relation between the mind and the existing thing. Since the same mode of being need not be present in both terms of the cognitive relation, there is no repugnance in maintaining both the distinction between the real to-be and the to-be-perceived, and also the intelligibility of the real act of existing and its actually being known in the existential judgment. Indeed, the act of existing can be rendered present in the knower, only on condition that the existential judgment affirm, at least implicitly, the real otherness between the act of judging and the act of being.

3. THE POLEMIC AGAINST MATTER

In the subtitle to his *Principles of Human Knowledge,* Berkeley proposed to inquire into "the chief causes of error and difficulty in the sciences, with the grounds of scepticism, atheism, and irreligion." This program characterized his entire approach to philosophical problems, since his constant concern was for the fate of common-sense beliefs and religious truths, in an age when skepticism, atheism, and irreligion were coming into the intellectual ascendancy. He believed that they could all be refuted together, and that the key to their common refutation lay in the *rejection of matter,* as a real entity.[12] Bayle's *Dictionary* had spread the attitude of Pyrrhonian *skepticism*

---

[12] *The Principles of Human Knowledge,* I, 86–96 (*Works,* II, 78–82). By way of clarification of the lines of battle, Berkeley adds: "The question between the materialists and me is not, whether things have a real existence out of the mind of this or that person, but whether they have an absolute existence, distinct from being perceived by God, and exterior to all minds." *Three Dialogues between Hylas and Philonous,* III (*Works,* II, 235). By posing the problem of the existence of material substance in this way, however, he precluded the possibility that this substance can be at once totally dependent upon God, completely known by Him, and also endowed by Him with an act of existing that is distinct from the act of being known by either God or finite minds. For Berkeley's central preoccupation with finding a refutation for skepticism, cf. R. H. Popkin, "Berkeley and Pyrrhonism," *The Review of Metaphysics,* 5 (1950–1951), 223–246.

by claiming that, if we can know only our own ideas directly, there is no certain way of coming to know a world distinct from these ideas and lying behind them. But if it can be shown that there is no material substance lying in the dark, then to know our own ideas is to have a perfectly evident and sure grasp upon the only real world: that of sensible things or ideas of sense. Again, *atheism* rests upon the view that the material universe is self-existent and hence requires no support from a God. But if the true situation is that matter is completely nonexistent and that the world of sensible bodies is a world of mind-dependent ideas, based ultimately upon the infinite spirit, then the grounds of atheism are removed. Finally, *irreligious materialism* will be unable to identify the first principle of the world with matter, if it is made manifest that all sensible existents are ideas and, as such, require the existence of a divine mind or immaterial substance. Hence, in his criticism of matter, Berkeley found a way of removing the greatest errors of his age, and of doing so in terms of the world view that most appealed to him. This double advantage sharpened the edge of his logical tools, when he applied them to the concept of matter.

The attempt of Locke and Malebranche to refute the above errors by means of their doctrine on matter is, in Berkeley's eyes, a total failure. In their philosophy, *matter* is:

> an inert, senseless substance, in which extension, figure, and motion, do actually subsist. . . . The matter philosophers contend for, is an incomprehensible somewhat which has none of those particular qualities, whereby the bodies falling under our senses are distinguished one from another. . . . It neither acts, nor perceives, nor is perceived.[13]

It is against this notion of matter that all of Berkeley's arguments are directed, and no alternative view is considered. If the direct objects of perception are ideas, we can know only ourselves as having this or that sensation or idea. Granted that ideas can only be like other ideas, the following dilemma develops: either matter must be reduced to the

---

[13] *The Principles of Human Knowledge,* I, 9, 47, 68 (*Works,* II, 44–45, 60, 70; spelling modernized). Although Malebranche did not deny the existence of matter, he held it on faith, rather than on reason, and explained matter in such a way as to prepare for Berkeley's outright denial; cf. A. D. Fritz, "Malebranche and the Immaterialism of Berkeley," *The Review of Metaphysics,* 3 (1949–1950), 59–80. Berkeley's immaterialism and Hume's phenomenalism are regarded, respectively, as a metaphysical and a skeptical solution to the Cartesian impasse over substance-and-modification, in two articles by R. A. Watson: "Berkeley in a Cartesian Context," *Revue Internationale de Philosophie,* 17 (1963), 381–394, and "The Breakdown of Cartesian Metaphysics," *Journal of the History of Philosophy,* 1 (1963), 177–197.

status of an idea, in order to be known, or else it must be placed entirely beyond our knowledge. In respect to sensible things, we cannot go beyond our ideas and hence cannot attain to a material substance which, by definition, lies beyond the relation between the perceiver and his ideas. If material substance is banished beyond knowledge, there is no rational ground for supposing its existence.

The burden of proof is thus laid upon those who make some positive affirmation about matter. They may answer that, although material substance is unknowable in itself, it can be known in its *relation with the qualities.* To meet the argument that matter is required at least as the support of qualities, Berkeley reviews the nature of these supposed modes of matter. He exploits the received distinction between primary and secondary qualities, since it already grants one half of his thesis. To hold that ordinary secondary qualities have only a subjective reality, is to concede the point that they exist only as ideas or objects-in-perception. All that remains for Berkeley to show is that there is *no essential epistemological difference between primary and secondary qualities.*[14] Hence the former must be considered just as mind-dependent as the latter. *All* qualities have their reality only as ideas related objectively to the percipient mind.

Extension, figure, motion, and solidity are reckoned by Locke among the primary qualities. But Berkeley appeals to the testimony of experience, that these aspects are never presented *in isolation* from the other properties of bodies. What is actually perceived, is not extension alone or motion alone but rather this extended, moving, colored, tangible thing. We are confronted with a *sensible whole:* if one group of its components are ideas in and for the perceiver, the same sort of being must be assigned to the remaining components. The argument about the relativity of ordinary secondary qualities to the perceiver can be extended to the primary qualities. Just as the color and taste of a thing vary with the subjective condition of the perceiver, so do the texture and shape and velocity. To the same person at different times or to several simultaneous observers, placed at different perspectives, the same object may appear now as small, smooth, and round; now as large, uneven, and angular. Solidity is easily reducible to a datum of touch and hence to an idea of sense.

The only recourse left for Berkeley's opponents is to distinguish

---

[14] For this dialectic, read *The Principles of Human Knowledge,* I, 9-15 (*Works,* II, 44-47); *Three Dialogues between Hylas and Philonous,* I (*Works,* II, 175-192); *Alciphron,* IV, 8-10 (*Works,* III, 150-154).

between *particular,* variable instances of extension, figure, and motion and the *absolute,* general nature of these properties "considered in themselves." As a countermove, Berkeley recalls his attack upon abstract, general ideas. The separation of extension as such from particular instances of extended bodies is an instance of vicious abstraction. Similarly, the uncoupling of primary from secondary qualities is due to an invalid abstraction from the integrity of concrete experience. Apart from particular sensible ideas, there are no existent qualities.

As a consequence, material substance is left literally existing *no-where* and supporting *no-thing.* The sensible thing or bodily complexus of qualities is not self-existent. But since its entire reality is that of a group of ideas, it finds its entire support *in the perceiving mind.* The mind has the qualities, in the only way in which they can be "had": as objects in and for the perceiver. On the other hand, "for an idea [i.e., a sensible quality] to exist in an unperceiving thing, is a manifest contradiction; for to have an idea is all one as to perceive: that therefore wherein colour, figure, and the like qualities exist, must perceive them; hence it is clear there can be no unthinking substance or *substratum* of those ideas."[15] Robbed of its supporting function and relation to the qualities, material substance shrivels up to a completely vacuous concept. Since it would be distinct from extension, it could not even conform to the vulgar view of material substance, as something spread out under the qualities or as an undergirding for them. Apart from these images, however, a material *substrate* is meaningless.

The remaining avenues of escape from complete immaterialism are easily blocked off. One of these would be the argument that, despite the impotence of the senses in regard to substance, it can nevertheless be apprehended by pure intelligence or reason. Berkeley's retort is that, if this be so, matter can have nothing in common with the bodies of our experience, since the latter are nothing more than *sensible* things or objects of sense imagination. As Locke admits, the purely rational view of substance-as-such resolves itself into the concept of *being* in general plus the function of *supporting* modes or

---

[15] *The Principles of Human Knowledge,* I, 7 (*Works,* II, 44). If one gives a "soft" meaning to matter, however, and identifies it with Berkeley's definition of the sensible thing, then he will not quibble about words but will admit it into his immaterialism; cf. *Three Dialogues between Hylas and Philonous,* III (*Works,* II, 261–262).

accidents. In the case of material substance, the supporting function has been eliminated, in view of the subjective nature of all sensible qualities. As for being or something in general, Berkeley terms it "the most abstract and incomprehensible of all" ideas,[16] since it evacuates all particular modes and instances of things. This comment on the concept of being as such is a clear indication that Berkeley's purview extends only to the Lockean version of abstraction as a total evacuation. Berkeley thinks that being is abstracted in the same way as the universal concepts, and merely carries the total abstraction to its limits. He fails to consider whether the metaphysical notion of being may not have a distinctive origin that cannot be reduced to the abstractive process, whether vicious or legitimate.

If matter does not vanish in a cloud of empty words, it is the locus of a flagrant set of contradictions. Material substance is supposed to be *inert,* and yet to be the *cause* of ideas in us. How matter could affect mind (especially within the Cartesian and Malebranchean dualism of substances) is just as inconceivable as how an idea could be compared with a nonmental kind of being. Matter is supposed to be *unperceiving* and yet to possess qualities, i.e., ideas, whose mode of existence is *to be perceived* by mind. On Locke's own reckoning, material substance has no necessary connection with its qualities, and nevertheless the latter are said to give some information about matter, at least enough to conclude that such a substance exists and has a certain function, as an underpinning. To sum up in one statement this congeries of contradictory predicates: matter is said to have *absolute existence apart from the mind.*[17] But the whole burden of Berkeley's reflections is that only minds and their idea-objects exist, and that it is illegitimate to separate sensible existence from the condition of being perceived by mind.

The success of Berkeley's argument depends, however, upon the soundness of the commonly held seventeenth-century thesis concerning the subjectivity of the secondary qualities. The Galilean doctrine on secondary and primary qualities was *methodologically* useful for securing the mathematical interpretation of the material world, but the progressive empiricist criticism revealed its inadequacy as a general philosophical tool. After Berkeley's critique, the problem of secondary and primary qualities became a peripheral one, since nonmathematical principles of interpretation came to the fore.

---

[16] *The Principles of Human Knowledge,* I, 17 (*Works,* II, 48); cf. *Three Dialogues between Hylas and Philonous,* III (*Works,* II, 237).

[17] *The Principles of Human Knowledge,* I, 24 (*Works,* II, 51).

Berkeley consigns matter to the lumber room of useless philosophical concepts. This is an overhasty dismissal. The only certain conclusion that follows from his dialectical analysis is that there is a serious conflict between Locke's notion of matter and Locke's doctrine on ideas and the proper philosophical method. Largely for the sake of securing an advantage over skepticism, atheism, and irreligious materialism, Berkeley sacrifices matter and yet retains the more basic Lockean conception of philosophical method and its object, the idea. Accepting this residue of empiricism, he has no other choice than to pose the problem of matter exclusively as a *problem concerning perception*. When the question is formulated solely in terms of the conditions of perception, it is not surprising that the answer should also be one in which sensible existence is reduced to the condition of being perceived by and in the mind. Now, this way of framing the issue excludes, beforehand, any doctrine of matter as a real principle of being. Hence Berkeley proves, not that the idea is the only sensible existent, but that a starting point in the analysis of ideas can tell nothing about the act of existing, exercised by material things. Either the analysis of ideas must be accepted integrally, and the elimination of real principles of being carried through even more radically than in the Berkeleyan polemic against matter, or else the empirical method and starting point must be subjected to a fundamental criticism. Hume accepts the first horn of this dilemma, whereas Kant explores one aspect of the second.

4. THE REALITY OF THE SENSIBLE WORLD

Seventy years after the publication of the *Principles of Human Knowledge*, Kant (with an eye to the critics of his own theory of space and time) gave classic expression to the charge that Berkeley's immaterialism destroys the objective world. According to Kant, Berkeley reduces natural things to subjective states and eventually to sheer illusion. This criticism was anticipated and most vigorously rejected by Berkeley himself, some of whose contemporaries likewise charged him with professing a doctrine of illusionism. Berkeley's rejoinder is that, quite on the contrary, his doctrine alone leaves intact and even reinforces the common-sense view of the world. His arguments are intended only to expel the sophisticated philosophical doctrine of *matter:* they vindicate the ordinary man's conceptions about *real bodies* or *sensible things*.[18] The latter remain exactly what

18 *Ibid.*, I, 35 (*Works*, II, 55); *Three Dialogues between Hylas and Philonous*, III

they are, but the mind is enabled now to slough off the false speculations of philosophers about a hidden material substance. The ordinary man believes that the objects of his immediate perception are the real things. Berkeley heartily agrees with this conviction — but he adds that the real things immediately perceived are ideas, and that there is no material existent, apart from our mental objects. In this way, the "vulgar" and the "philosophical" views of sensible reality are reconciled. But his agreement with, and defense of, common-sense realism is of a quite critical and, in its own way, sophisticated sort. The real world of common sense stays intact, within the Berkeleyan vision of things, only on condition that "reality" is brought in line with the New Principle. For Berkeley as well as Leibniz, the common-sense outlook must be transformed, not simply accepted.

Berkeley offers a systematic reinterpretation of three notes that are usually attached to the sensible order of being: its reality, its distinctness from the perceiver, and its permanent existence.

1. The only available criterion of *reality* is found within the order of ideas themselves or, rather, in their various relations to the mind.[19] The distinction between ideas of sense and ideas of imagination is again invoked by Berkeley. The human mind is receptive in respect to *ideas of sense,* whereas it is the originative source of *ideas of imagination.* The understanding can frame images at will, but it must simply accept sensory ideas as they are given. This fundamental difference of relation between the mind and these two classes of ideas cannot be erased. It is confirmed by an analysis of the ideas themselves. By comparison with sense perceptions, ideas of imagination are weak, faint, unsteady, and incoherent. On the contrary, there is a characteristic strength, liveliness, distinctness, and order about ideas of sense. This contrast may be used as a criterion of the reality of sensible things or ideas of sense. As effects impressed upon our mind directly by God, they have a special claim to more reality than the ideas derived from our invention and combination. Ideas of sense constitute the real order, the *rerum natura,* whereas ideas of imagination are either likenesses of this given reality or chimeras of our own framing. Although dependent upon the divine will, ideas of sense

---

(*Works,* II, 262). For Kant's opinion of Berkeley, cf. *Prolegomena to Any Future Metaphysics,* 13, Remark, and the Appendix (L. W. Beck's revision of the Carus translation, 41, 123–125).

[19] *The Principles of Human Knowledge,* I, 29, 30, 33–36, 90–91 (*Works,* II, 53–56, 80–81); *Three Dialogues between Hylas and Philonous,* II (*Works,* II, 215).

are not products of our human will, and cannot be called mere chimeras or free constructions of our mind. This accounts for the common distinction between the real and the imaginary.

2. The skeptical retort would be that both real and imaginary objects agree in being ideas, and hence in being mere subjective modifications of the mind. Berkeley accepted their ideal nature but not the inference that they are mere subjective modifications. The more he read in contemporary philosophy, the more he became convinced that the customary pairing of substance and mode would have to be abandoned, especially if any answer were to be made to skepticism and the materialism of Hobbes (with whom he associated Spinoza, for attributing extension to God). In addition to the refutation of material substance, it became necessary for Berkeley to eliminate the view that ideas are *modes* of the mind, whether divine or human. Ideas are *objects* of the mind's perceiving operation and in this sense alone are they in the mind. "Those qualities are in the mind only as they are perceived by it, that is, not by way of *mode* or *attribute,* but only by way of *idea.*"[20] This nonmodal sort of mental presence of ideas of sense guarantees the *objectivity* of sensible things. Hence they cannot be regarded as mere subjective modifications. The sensible world is also *really distinct* from the perceiver, in the sense that there is a real distinction between the mind and the objects of the mind, between perceiving and being perceived. Furthermore, the dependence of sensible things or ideas upon the human understanding is accidental, rather than essential. We cannot specify, at will, the structure of ideas of sense. They are essentially dependent only upon the divine mind and will. The sensible world is neither a mode nor a product of the human mind, and hence there is a basis in immaterialism for the common-sense belief in the objectivity and distinctness of the world. Berkeley even allowed that the sensible world is *external,* insofar as sensible things or ideas may exist apart from my individual mind, even though their existence is confined to the minds of other finite perceivers or God.

3. Berkeley foresaw the Humean objection that, if the existence of ideas is one with their being perceived, then (at least, for all we can know) the sensible world ceases to exist, whenever the acts of perception themselves cease. This would lead to the doctrine of inter-

---

[20] *The Principles of Human Knowledge,* I, 49 (*Works,* II, 61); cf. *Three Dialogues between Hylas and Philonous,* III (*Works,* II, 237). On difficulties in the phrase: "in the mind," see E. B. Allaire, "Berkeley's Idealism," *Theoria,* 29 (1963), 229–244.

mittent existence and a consequent denial of the *permanence* of sense things. Berkeley struggled with this objection from several angles.[21] He assumed a position closer to Leibniz than to Locke, concerning whether the mind ever ceases to perceive. If the nature of the mind is nothing other than to be an active center of willing and perceiving, then it continues to will and perceive in some degree, as long as it exists. Its own existence is a temporal process, one that supposes a continuous flow of volitions and ideas, and hence continuous acts of willing and perceiving. Although Berkeley did not develop a detailed theory, corresponding to Leibniz' doctrine on the minute, unconscious perceptions, he did give distinctive emphasis to the volitional or appetitive side of the life of the mind.

An objection can be made that, however continuous the perceiving operation, it does not always have *these* particular sensible things as its objects, and hence that uninterrupted perception of some sort does not guarantee the continuance in existence of *these* particular sensible things. This criticism forced Berkeley to appeal to the distinction between God's mind and our own (and thus to make the problem of our knowledge of God a central problem for Hume, even in regard to an analysis of the sensible world). Sensible things depend essentially and constantly upon the divine mind, which always actually wills and perceives them. When they are not being perceived by one individual finite mind, they *may* be perceived by some other human mind and *must* be perceived and willed by the divine intelligence. The sense world does not alternately come to be and cease to be, in rhythm with individual human perceptions, since the unconditional ground of its existence is its permanent status as an object of *God's unfailing actual perception* and *volition*.

Within the human perspective, however, a distinction does obtain

---

[21] *The Principles of Human Knowledge*, I, 45, 48, 98 (*Works*, II, 59, 61, 83–84). The genesis of this doctrine can be traced in the following entries in *Philosophical Commentaries*: 41, 52, 282, 472–473, 478, 791, 802, 812 (*Works*, I, 11, 13, 35, 59, 60, 95, 96, 97). When he remains at the finite plane of analysis, Berkeley comes close to making the existence of sense things depend solely upon our power to perceive and will them, or even upon our power to imagine them. In order to establish a firm distinction between the real and the imaginary, he must understand the New Principle strictly in terms of actual perception and must ground this actual perception in the divine mind. In "The Place of God in Berkeley's Philosophy," *Philosophy*, 6 (1931), 18–29, J. D. Mabbott brings out the indispensable role of God, but he sets up a needless conflict between God as perceiver and God as willer. Berkeley retains both functions in God, although his view that there is a passive aspect in perception raised a special problem, for him, of how to attribute cognition to God.

between *the perceived* and *the perceivable*. Berkeley exploits it in a skillful way, to meet the objection about intermittent existence. For, that which is only perceivable to one man may be actually perceived by another man, and must be perceived and willed by God. It may be inquired, however, whether this distinction does not make a breach in the system of immaterialism. Since a sensible thing may nevertheless be actually existing, even on the extreme hypothesis of its being the object of no human perception whatsoever, there would seem to be a clear case of a real distinction between *esse* and *percipi*. Berkeley's response to this difficulty is not entirely satisfactory. He remarks that this distinction does not obtain in every respect. When the object is only potentially perceived by human observers, its claim to real existence is founded upon its actual perception by God. In the extreme instance, then, the gap between existing and being actually perceived is closed, only on the supposition of God's actual, ceaseless perception and volition of the thing. Whatever the legitimacy of an *eventual* appeal to the divine knowledge, however, it cannot serve as a proper defense of the New Principle, considered precisely as the *first* principle in the immaterialist philosophy.[22] For, Berkeley's proof of God's existence and nature depends, in turn, upon the implications that can be drawn from this principle, once its truth is established. Hence, if circular reasoning is to be avoided, the principle itself cannot be defended in terms of one of its consequences. For this reason, Berkeley's usual practice is to establish his principle in respect to actual perception of sensible things, and to give special treatment to the question of perceivability only as an answer to the difficulty about intermittent existence. But this procedure conceals the extent of the circular dependence of his theory of knowledge upon an implicit theory of the divine mind.

5. THE REALM OF MINDS

Despite his defense of the reality of the sensible world and the

---

[22] In a helpful survey and criticism of the various arguments adduced by Berkeley in defense of his immaterialism, J. P. de C. Day ("George Berkeley, 1685–1753," *The Review of Metaphysics*, 6 [1952–1953], 83–113, 265–286, 447–469, 583–596), shows that the distinction between the perceivable and the perceived is ultimately of no avail to Berkeley as an epistemological foundation, since he wishes to preserve his system from illusionism. Hence he must invoke God's actual perception of objects. In doing so, however, he makes the divine perception both the ground and the consequent of his New Principle.

basic reliability of the common-sense outlook, Berkeley often refers to the objects of perception as *ideas,* rather than as *things.*[23] He offers two main reasons for this usage. First, although ideas of sense are the things comprising the sensible world, nevertheless in the popular mind "thing" conveys the meaning of an entity *existing absolutely* or without relation of dependence on any mind. By speaking primarily about sense ideas, Berkeley removes the presumption in favor of a self-contained material world, as well as Locke's anxiety about how to compare sensory likenesses with independently existing things. Another reason for preferring "idea" to "thing" is that "thing" is a wider term. The domain of things contains two broad classes: *ideas* and *minds.* Ideas are sensible things, but there are other things, viz., minds, that are something more than objects of perception. Since minds are not the same as ideas, it would be misleading to use "thing" exclusively as a synonym for "idea."

Berkeley's doctrine on *mind* is constructed mainly by way of contrast with ideas or objects of perception. The three natures to which human knowledge attains are: ideas of sense, ideas of imagination, and minds (the latter being grasped by attending to our internal operations).[24] If the *esse* of ideas is *percipi,* the *esse* of mind is *percipere.* Whereas ideas as such are passive and inert, minds are essentially active and causal. Ideas are fleeting, dependent, and perishable; minds are enduring, subsisting, and incorruptible. In the sensible order, there is no substance; the only substances are immaterial ones, i.e., minds or spirits. None of the reasons that tell against material substance can be transferred to a critique of *immaterial substance.* There are no intrinsic contradictions in the latter conception. For, a spirit is neither an inert cause nor an unperceiving bearer of ideas nor an unperceivable, bodily thing.

---

[23] *The Principles of Human Knowledge,* I, 38–39 (*Works,* II, 56–57); *Three Dialogues between Hylas and Philonous,* III (*Works,* II, 235–236). Berkeley substitutes "things" for "ideas" in certain contexts, so that it will seem less "harsh and ridiculous" that we should eat and drink *ideas.* For the sake of ordinary sensibilities, one should say: we eat and drink the *things* immediately perceived by our senses. This is an instance where Berkeley follows the maxim that "we ought to *think with the learned, and speak with the vulgar.*" *The Principles of Human Knowledge,* I, 51 (*Works,* II, 62; the editor of this volume traces the quotation to a sixteenth-century Italian, Augustinus Niphus, and notes that Bacon also used it).

[24] This interpretation of *ibid.,* I, 1 (*Works,* II, 41) follows the reading suggested by A. A. Luce, *Berkeley's Immaterialism,* 39–40.

BERKELEY'S IMMATERIALIST UNIVERSE

1. God, the infinite mind or spirit (unlimited, immaterial substance or personal self, whose to-be is to-perceive and to-will: pure creative activity).

2. Men, finite minds or spirits (limited, immaterial substances or personal selves, whose to-be is to-perceive and to-will, but with reception of their being, power to act, and ideas from God).

3. Contents of finite minds.
   a) Ideas of sense: the nonmaterial, nonsubstantial world of real sensible things, communicated to finite minds by God, according to orderly, settled patterns (the natural laws of the sensible world).
   b) Ideas of imagination: produced by the wills of finite minds.
   c) Notions: the cognitive means for knowing minds, activities, and relations.

To establish the existence of spiritual substances, Berkeley appeals to familiar experience. We refer meaningfully to ourselves as perceiving agents, by way of contrast with our percepts. That which does the perceiving, willing, and imagining, enjoys a mode of being distinct from the things perceived, willed, and imagined. Hence "by the word *spirit* [or *mind*] we mean only that which thinks, wills, and perceives."[25] It is to this immaterial substance that the ideas are said to belong, and in which they are said to be present as objects. In regarding the *mind* or *self* as a *substance,* Berkeley rejects the Lockean phenomenalistic view of the self and provides, in advance, an answer to Hume's contention that the self is a floating system of ideas. "I know that I, one and the same self, perceive both colours and sounds: that a colour cannot perceive a sound, nor a sound a colour: that I am therefore one individual principle, distinct from colour and sound; and, for the same reason, from all other sensible things and inert ideas."[26] Berkeley traces the purely phenomenalistic view of the

---

[25] *The Principles of Human Knowledge,* I, 138 (*Works,* II, 104); cf. *ibid.,* I, 27, 135–139 (*Works,* II, 52–53, 103–105), on the nature of mind or spirit. The characteristic activity of minds is discussed by A. Leroy, "Remarques sur l'activité des esprits dans la philosophie berkeleyenne," *Revue Philosophique de la France et de l'Étranger,* 135 (1945), 256–272.

[26] *Three Dialogues between Hylas and Philonous,* III (*Works,* II, 233–234). A series of entries, often cited from *Philosophical Commentaries* (*Works,* I, 72–73) as proof of Berkeley's own early phenomenalism of self, should rather be taken as a dialogue between Berkeley and a Lockean, who assumes that all words have corresponding ideas and that only ideas are the direct objects of our knowledge.

self to the twin assumptions that there are no words without corresponding ideas, and that we can know only that of which we can have ideas. On the contrary, to the word "self," there corresponds a spiritual substance, rather than an idea. And, in order to locate the mind in the substantial order, he is now forced to deny that we have any *idea* of the mind or substantial self. On the principle that an idea can be the likeness only of another idea, it follows that there can be no idea of the mind, which is defined by contrast with the characteristics of ideas or sensible things.

In one sense, then, the mind is unknowable: it cannot be known through ideas. But its existence is nevertheless a primary deliverance of consciousness. This forces Berkeley to posit a new means of knowledge, essentially different from the idea. This is the reason for his fundamental distinction between *idea* and *notion*.[27] The latter is the instrument for grasping those things that lie beyond the domain of ideas: one's own self, other minds, actions, and relations. Moreover, since one's mind is not a sensible thing, the manner of apprehending it must also differ from that of apprehending sensible things. It can be seized by oneself only intuitively, in the very act of willing and perceiving. Berkeley employs the language of Malebranche, in referring to this immediate apprehension of the substantial self as an *inward feeling* or *reflection*. Yet he makes no detailed analysis of this cardinal operation, simply continuing the tradition of Descartes that we do have an intuitive understanding of our own substantial self. Both "notion" and "inward feeling" are regarded by Berkeley as imperfect ways of transcribing an undeniable experience of knowing an immaterial, substantial, personal self. But in Hume's view, they are *ad hoc* inventions, made in order to avoid his own doctrine on the self. Berkeley contributes to this judgment, insofar as he devotes nowhere near the amount of circumstantial analysis to the knowledge of the self, as he does to the knowledge of the qualities.

The mind or personal self is an active reality, containing *understanding* and *will*.[28] The relation of these latter perfections to the spiritual substance became a troublesome issue for Berkeley. His two

---

[27] See J. W. Davis, "Berkeley's Doctrine of the Notion," *The Review of Metaphysics*, 12 (1958–1959), 378–389; S. M. Najm, "Knowledge of the Self in Berkeley's Philosophy," *International Philosophical Quarterly*, 6 (1966), 248–269.

[28] *Philosophical Commentaries*, 643, 645, 674, 713, 841, 848 (*Works*, I, 79, 82, 87, 100, 101); *The Principles of Human Knowledge*, I, 27, 143 (*Works*, II, 52–53, 106–107).

chief difficulties concerned the active nature of the understanding and the general theory of mental powers. On the first problem, his early speculations were considerably influenced by the views of Descartes and Locke concerning the passive character of the understanding. Hence, he tended to erect a sharp contrast between understanding and will, taken respectively as the passive and active sides of the mind. But there was a twofold inconvenience about considering the understanding as a purely passive power: to do so, would be to break down the difference between the active mind and its passive ideas, and also to wipe out the basis for a difference between the operations of willing and perceiving. Hence Berkeley finally concluded that, although the finite understanding has a *passive* aspect (insofar as it receives ideas from God), it is not entirely inert but also has an *active* aspect (insofar as it actually perceives the ideas it does receive). As for the theory of mental powers, Berkeley suspected that it rests upon a vicious abstraction. Since Locke treated understanding and will as abstract ideas, Berkeley concluded that the power theory always results in the hypostasization of the various faculties of the mind and thus destroys the indivisible unity of mental life. Consequently, he preferred to regard understanding and will as *functional aspects* of the mind, rather than as *powers,* in the Lockean sense. The understanding is nothing other than the mind, considered as perceiving given ideas of sense; the will is nothing other than the mind, now considered as forming new ideas of imagination or as ordering something in respect to our ideas. Since these two functions are mutually ordained and convergent in nature, the mind or spirit is the actual concretion of perception and volition.

Despite his restricted historical appreciation of the meaning of a mental power, Berkeley does show a keen awareness of the concrete unity of mental life and the interpenetration of knowing and willing. Yet he is prevented from resolving the issues he raises, both because he confines his analysis to the Lockean view of powers and because his own New Principle is better fitted for dealing with *things* (in Berkeley's system: minds and ideas) than with *principles of being.* That is why the results of Berkeleyan analysis fall just short of being metaphysical explanations of finite reality. In the case of powers of the mind, he is confronted with anomalies, which can be reduced neither to mind-thing nor to idea-thing. He is right in refusing to reify the powers, but not in refusing them any metaphysical status. He cannot account for powers of the mind, because of the limitations of his New Principle, which does not recognize that these powers are *principles whereby* the concrete substance itself achieves its operational perfection. Thus, the opportunity is lost to provide a solid metaphysical basis for his conviction about the dynamic unity of mental life and the need for a subordinate principle of unity, integrating the personal substance and its operations. The metaphysical theory of powers performs this function, but it does so, only by regarding the powers, operations, and substance of man in terms of act and potency. The thing-bound New Principle of Berkeley is essentially unfitted to perform an analysis of powers as operative principles, within the unity of human nature.

The only strictly immediate knowledge is that of one's own mind and perceptual contents. Berkeley tries his best to avoid the *solipsistic* implications of this description of the cognitive situation. He bases his escape from solipsism mainly upon the demonstration of *God's existence*.[29] He announces that immaterialism provides the only definitive answer to atheism, since it alone offers a proof of God's existence which is both intelligible to the average man and yet strictly demonstrative. Once more, Berkeley makes use of the distinction between ideas of sense and ideas of imagination. The latter can be produced by the finite mind, employing its own active power of will. But our mind is passive, in respect to the content of the ideas of sense. Perceiving is an operation of the mind, but *what* we perceive lies beyond our control. Some other active principle must be invoked, in order to account for the actual presentation of sensory contents to our mind, since we cannot voluntarily determine this content. Now, the sole source of the ideas of sense is some voluntary, spiritual principle. These ideas cannot come from material substance, the existence of which has been disproven. Nor can sensible things (as defined by Berkeley) be responsible for these ideas. For, there is no real distinction between ideas of sense and sensible things; consequently, sensible things partake of the inert, causally inefficacious character of all ideas. The active source of the ideas of sense is some spiritual substance. It is not a finite, spiritual substance, since the active principle must be powerful enough to convey to the finite mind the entire order of nature, which is nothing more than the regulated

---

[29] For the demonstration, see *ibid.*, I, 146–149 (*Works*, II, 107–109); *Three Dialogues between Hylas and Philonous*, II (*Works*, II, 211–215); *Alciphron*, IV, 2–5 (*Works*, III, 142–148). For the problem of solipsism, consult D. Grey, "The Solipsism of Bishop Berkeley," *The Philosophical Quarterly*, 2 (1951–1952), 338–349.

series of ideas of sense. The order and variety of these ideas manifest the existence of an infinite, spiritual substance or mind, having intelligence and will. The ideas of sense must have their primary being as objects in an infinite mind, and must be communicated to us through a deliberate, intelligent act of volition, on the part of the first principle. The *personal* nature of God is an immediate consequence of the presence of infinite will and understanding, as aspects of His spiritual being.

The question of the relationship between the New Principle and the existence of God has already been raised, in connection with the problem of intermittent existence. Berkeley relies implicitly upon the existence of God, as an infinite and actual perceiver, in order to secure the identification between sensible *esse* and *percipi*. Unless the constant, actual, divine perception is presupposed, Berkeley cannot avoid the Humean consequence of foregoing any assurance about the permanence or continuity-in-existence of sensible things. The capital distinction between what is strictly perceivable and what is only imaginable by us, is secured only by measuring the *humanly perceivable* by the implicit standard of what *God actually perceives*. But this means that the New Principle itself both serves as the basis for the proof of God's existence and stands in need of His existence for its own foundation. Furthermore, as Hume and Kant later pointed out, Berkeley's appeal to the totality of nature, as proof of the infinity of the active source of our ideas of sense, leads only to a very powerful orderer, not necessarily to an infinite mind. Berkeley's principles of inference are not sufficiently founded in the finite act of existing to enable him to reach the infinite act of existing.

In considering how a finite mind can gain some knowledge of God's infinite nature, Berkeley consulted many traditional treatises on the divine names. He mentioned the views of Dionysius the Pseudo-Areopagite, Aquinas, Cajetan, and Suarez. He applauded Cajetan's distinction between metaphorical and proper analogy, for our knowledge of God is more than a genial guess or metaphor. Although he agreed with Cajetan that our knowledge of God is according to the *analogy of proper proportionality,* Berkeley was prevented by his own method and starting point from appropriating the content of this doctrine on analogical predication. The fundamental metaphysical obstacle was his view that, although "*thing* or *being* is the most general name of all, it comprehends under it two kinds entirely distinct and heterogeneous, and which have nothing

common but the name, to wit, *spirits* and *ideas*."[30] This theory did
not permit sufficient analogical unity to provide a basis for analogy
of proper proportionality. But Berkeley did offer a concrete description of the human mind's operation, in reasoning about God's nature.
The finite mind removes the imperfections present in itself, and then
heightens its own perfections, thus following the ways of negation
and eminence. It uses its own intuited nature as a sort of image or
mirror, in which to spy something about the nature of an infinitely
perfect spiritual substance, having understanding and will. Only a
far-off glimpse of the infinite spirit is gained in this way, but of
his existence and personal providence we have complete assurance.

Berkeley does not display the same confidence about proving the
existence of *other finite minds*.[31] He never doubts the fact of their
existence, but neither does he claim that we can come to know this
fact with the same certainty that marks our knowledge of God.
Sufficiently cogent grounds for the belief in other minds are found,
however, to warrant calling the argument a demonstration. I seem
to receive certain ideas as a result of bodily motions, apparently
originating from another agent, at my own finite level of being.
When the mouth I see before me moves, and words are spoken and
heard, ideas are then aroused in my mind that correspond to the
very ideas I would intend to evoke, through the use of similar
bodily gestures and words. I can conclude, with high likelihood,
that these received ideas are communicated to me, in view of the
intentions of another finite spirit. I may take such ideas as signs
of the presence of other finite minds, who are constituted like myself.

Although he calls this argument a demonstration, Berkeley admits
that the evidence does not permit of a strict causal proof. The

---

[30] *The Principles of Human Knowledge*, I, 89 (*Works*, II, 79); cf. *ibid.*, I, 142
(*Works*, II, 106). This sharp contrast between spirits and ideas is an attempt to stress
(against Malebranche) both the objectivity of ideas and their objective presence in
and for finite minds, which exercise causal operations of perceiving and willing, in
respect to their own ideas. We do not see all things in God, as Malebranche claimed,
but see the ideas in our own minds, and then reason to the existence and nature of
God. For these historical differences, cf. T. E. Jessop, "Malebranche and Berkeley,"
Revue Internationale de Philosophie, I (1938-1939), 121-142. On our analogical way
of knowing God, see *Three Dialogues between Hylas and Philonous*, III (*Works*, II,
230-232); *Alciphron*, IV, 19-21 (*Works*, III, 166-170).

[31] *The Principles of Human Knowledge*, I, 140, 145, 147-148 (*Works*, II, 105, 107,
108-109); *Three Dialogues between Hylas and Philonous*, III (*Works*, II, 231-233,
239-240); *Alciphron*, IV, 5 (*Works*, III, 146-147). Berkeley does not treat this problem
separately but interweaves it with his discussion of our knowledge of God.

bodily gestures, apparently existing in an independent entity, cannot be shown to be more than ideas belonging solely to my own mind. Furthermore, it is God alone who "maintains that intercourse between spirits, whereby they are able to perceive the existence of each other."[32] I can command the motions of my own bodily limbs and organs, but this only means that I can control the ideas of motion, as signs of my purpose. Like all other ideas, the *ideas of motion* are inert and causally inefficacious. God is required to produce in another mind the appropriate ideas, corresponding to what I intend by my bodily motions. The causal inference returns once more to God, the primary active principle, considered this time as the causal bridge between finite minds. To address another person means to have the intention to communicate with him, but to do so solely through God's communication of appropriate ideas of sense to that other person. Berkeley's interpretation of interpersonal communication is a strained one, and yet is required by his principles. Because he has defined spiritual substance mainly by contrast with sensible things and has reduced the latter to inert ideas, he has deprived incarnate human persons of any direct, active means of establishing relations and achieving mutual understanding.

Once the existence of several finite minds is established, the problem of *intersubjective knowledge* arises. The American philosopher, Samuel Johnson, posed the difficulty to Berkeley of how several men may be said to see the *same tree* or to agree upon any common piece of knowledge, since each individual mind has *different ideas* or *perceived objects*.[33] Berkeley distinguished between the vulgar and the philosophical meaning of identity, as applied to the question of identity of knowledge. He himself sided with the vulgar view that identity means absence of any perceptible difference. Thus there might be individual differences between the ideas in various minds, but as long as these differences remained unnoticed, the knowledge would be practically the same for all observers. Berkeley is hampered, by lack of a doctrine on intentional likeness, from establishing any stricter unity of agreement among the judgments pronounced by several minds, concerning the same existing thing. He appeals again to the divine mind, to furnish a safeguard for immaterialism against

---

32 *The Principles of Human Knowledge*, I, 147 (*Works*, II, 108).
33 For Johnson's question, cf. *Philosophical Correspondence between Berkeley and Samuel Johnson* (*Works*, II, 285–286); Berkeley's positive position is stated in *Three Dialogues between Hylas and Philonous*, III (*Works*, II, 247–248).

utter *relativism*. For although there is no independent, material referent for our individual ideas, the same function is fulfilled by the divine idea. The divine idea is the *archetypal pattern* and *essential measure* of all ideas in individual, finite minds. Hence it provides the basic sameness of meaning, that enables several minds to perceive the same thing and share the same knowledge. Because of this divine archetype for both our immediate perceptions and our reasoning, there can be objective truth and a science of nature, commonly known by many minds.

6. MIND AND NATURE

Throughout his writings, Berkeley was interested not only in refuting skepticism, atheism, and irreligious materialism but also in establishing the foundation and limits of the sciences. For, one major reason leading to the three former errors was a lack of precision concerning the proper province of mathematical and physical reasoning. Contemporary skepticism, for instance, flourished on the mathematical paradoxes concerning infinite divisibility. Berkeley challenged the assumption that the difficulties met with in mathematics are relevant grounds for casting suspicion upon the mind's ability to resolve philosophical issues.

Especially in his earlier years, he had an unbounded admiration for the demonstrative power of pure mathematics. But the more he became practiced in the empirical study of ideas and minds, the more clearly he saw that *mathematical* and *philosophical* demonstrations are of a different nature.[34] The former are purely analytic and (at least in reference to problems about spiritual and sensible existence) fall within the Lockean classification of trifling propositions. Philosophical reasoning is primarily concerned with the concrete, nonanalytic truths of coexistence, which are not susceptible of mathematical treatment and which also resist any philosophical treatment based on material substance. Berkeley stressed the nonexistential and basically practical orientation of mathematical thinking. The purpose of this emphasis is to ward off the inference that the mathematical paradoxes about extension and motion have any independent bearing upon the real nature of sensible things. These paradoxes do not show

---

[34] Berkeley's writings on mathematics are collected in Volume IV of the *Works*. He summarizes his position in *The Principles of Human Knowledge*, I, 118–132 (*Works*, II, 94–102).

that bodies are infinitely divisible, for in respect to the existing order
the conditions of perception must be respected. There is no quantitative reality beyond the range of perception, and hence we must
suppose that finite *minima sensibilia* are present, in the objects of
our senses. To the extent that Bayle and his skeptical followers
ignore the limitations of sense perception, they are dealing with purely
abstract, general ideas, and come to conclusions that have only verbal
significance. Such conclusions should not shake our confidence in the
mind's ability to reach truths about real, existential objects.

At the other extreme from abstract mathematics would be a purely
concrete physics, which might attempt to study the world, without
the use of mathematical techniques. Such a project would never make
progress, since it would be confined to a simple registration of sense
data and would never achieve scientific generalization. Genuine ad-
vances in the understanding of nature have been made by mechanics,
which applies mathematical reasoning to the field of sense objects.
Berkeley greatly admired Newton's combination of reason and observation, in the development of a *natural philosophy.* But he opposed the
pretentious claims being made by the Newtonians for this natural
or experimental philosophy, whether the claims were made in the
interest of religion or of irreligion.[35] For, the arguments rested upon

---

35 For Berkeley's views on Newton and the Newtonians, cf. *ibid.,* 101–117 (*Works,*
II, 85–94); *Three Dialogues between Hylas and Philonous,* III (*Works,* II, 257–258);
the entire opusculum, *De Motu* (*Works, IV,* 11–30); *Siris,* 285–293 (*Works,* V, 133–136).
Berkeley gives pithy expression to his limitation of natural philosophy, in a reply to the
American Samuel Johnson: "The true use and end of Natural Philosophy is to explain
the *phenomena of nature;* which is done by discovering the laws of nature, and reducing
particular appearances to them. This is Sir Isaac Newton's method; and such method or
design is not in the least inconsistent with the principles I lay down. This mechanical
philosophy does not assign or support any one *natural efficient cause* in the strict and
proper sense; nor is it, as to its use, concerned about *matter;* nor is matter connected
therewith; nor does it infer the being of matter." *Letter of November 25, 1729,* in
Philosophical Correspondence between Berkeley and Samuel Johnson (*Works,* II, 279;
italics added and spelling modernized). When these qualifications are respected, Berkeley
sees no conflict between his immaterialism and Newtonian natural philosophy. For a
logical positivist approach to Berkeley's theory of science, cf. G. Hinrichs, "The Logical
Positivism of Berkeley's *De Motu,*" *The Review of Metaphysics,* 3 (1949–1950),
491–505. Both Kant and Berkeley contrast the philosophical method with the analytic
procedure in mathematics. But, whereas Kant models philosophy after Newton's
natural philosophy, Berkeley refuses to pattern philosophical thinking after the
noncausal, nonexistential method of physics. See T. E. Jessop, "Berkeley and the Contemporary Physics," *Revue Internationale de Philosophie,* 7 (1953), 87–100. For
Berkeley's anticipation of Ernst Mach's famous criticism of Newtonian mechanics, cf.
the two articles by K. R. Popper and G. J. Whitrow, in *The British Journal for the
Philosophy of Science,* 4 (1953), 26–45.

an inadequate conception of the scope and limits of the Newtonian method, as well as upon careless references to natural powers, forces, and absolute entities. Although he did not propose to eliminate these latter references entirely from the study of nature, Berkeley did suggest a severe restriction of their meaning. They are useful in elaborating mathematical hypotheses, but they should not be mistaken for real efficient causes or things in nature. At most, the mathematical description of bodies provides a compendious way of computing, making practical plans, and teaching others. But the convenience of mechanical formulas is no indication that they express the real qualities and agencies of nature.

Only from the vantage point of immaterialism, can the restricted scope of mathematical physics be assessed. It studies *ideas* or *sensible phenomena* in themselves and their mathematically determinable connections. But natural science is prevented, in principle, from reaching the *true causes of physical events,* since it does not study the only causal agents at work in nature: minds or spiritual things. It is misleading to refer to mathematical equations and correlations as causal powers (as the incautious Newtonians did) or to describe bodies in terms of vital entelechies and spiritual forces (as Leibniz did). The world of bodies is an inert world of effects, containing no intrinsic, causal power. *Natural laws* are neither *causal* nor *necessary.*[36] They are not causal, since their content is restricted to "corporeal motions," i.e., to the ideas of motions. But even ideas of motions must submit to the general law that all ideas are inert, inactive objects of perception. One idea may follow regularly upon another, so that in an accommodated sense one may speak of the sequence as being one of natural cause and effect. But philosophically regarded, this sequence of ideas expresses only the relation between *sign* and *thing signified.* Hence there is no intrinsic, necessary connection between prior and subsequent things, in the series of natural events.

Berkeley was willing to concede to Malebranche that the sign or prior event may be called an "occasional cause," but it receives this name, only because it determines *our mental expectation* of the event that regularly follows it. Because our practical expectations depend upon the sequence of ideas of sense, God communicates these ideas to our minds according to a settled pattern, called the *order of nature.*

[36] *The Principles of Human Knowledge,* I, 30–32, 62–66, 150 (*Works,* II, 53–54, 67–70, 109); *Three Dialogues between Hylas and Philonous,* III (*Works,* II, 230–231); *Siris,* 254 (*Works,* V, 120–121).

Having deprived the Newtonian world of its autonomy and causal efficacy, Berkeley was now ready to defend its regularity. The stability of the order of nature consists entirely in the regular way God operates, in giving ideas to finite minds. The only kind of necessity attributable to natural laws is this derived necessity, imparted by God's customary action. And since the order of nature is intended as an aid to our practical planning, scientific laws have a *utilitarian* import for Berkeley: they are sufficiently probable to serve the purposes of human foresight and conduct. Berkeley followed Malebranche in making this appraisal of natural science, but he did not limit causal power to God. Having made no critical examination of cause as such or of its transcendental application to God, he was untroubled about the causal power of finite minds over their own ideas or about the stability of the natural order. But Berkeley's principles cut much deeper than he realized. For, they led him to strip sensible things of all real causal power and to reduce our conviction in natural causation to a subjective, probable expectation, aroused by custom and practical needs. These consequences led Hume to remark that, from Berkeley, one may glean "the best lessons of scepticism. . . . That all his arguments, though otherwise intended, are, in reality, merely sceptical, appears from this, *that they admit of no answer and produce no conviction.*"[37] Although there is some elegant satire behind this comment, it does convey accurately the actual effect which a reading of Berkeley's account of the order of nature and natural causation had upon the young Hume.

Berkeley's own intention, in making this reinterpretation of nature, was to arouse quite the contrary of a skeptical response in his readers. The Newtonian search after an absolute space, lurking behind perceptible, relative space; the indiscriminate application of the term "infinite" to large or small bodies, or even to abstract terms; the quest of causes, supposed to exist at the sensible level — these were among the tendencies in natural science of which he disapproved. He felt that their psychological effect was to turn the human mind away from contemplation of God and toward an exclusive study of

---

[37] David Hume, *An Enquiry concerning Human Understanding,* XII, 2 (Selby-Bigge edition, 155, n. 1). That Hume had only a minimal acquaintance with Berkeley, and hence that we should not take a closed view of the Anglo-Hibernian trio, Locke-Berkeley-Hume, is the warning contained in R. H. Popkin's articles: "Did Hume Ever Read Berkeley?" *The Journal of Philosophy,* 56 (1959), 535–545, and "So, Hume Did Read Berkeley," *The Journal of Philosophy,* 61 (1964), 773–778.

finite, sensible things. As a countermeasure, his own immaterialism presented another way of looking at nature, a way that did not stand in obscurantist opposition to the sciences but that opened up further religious prospects for our intelligence. Even in his early treatise, *A New Theory of Vision,* he had suggested that the objects of vision are not only ideas *for* the human mind but also messages *from* the divine mind. This view of sensible things deepened with Berkeley's detailed development of the theses on immaterialism. The theocentric interpretation of *nature as the language of God* marked the culmination of the religious tendency animating all his philosophical speculations.[38]

Berkeley agrees with Locke and Leibniz in rejecting the Malebranchean doctrine about seeing all things *in God.* The immediate objects of our perception remain the ideas *in our own mind,* together with our own mental operations. Nevertheless, we can habituate ourselves to see more in the objects of perception than the ideas themselves. Meditation upon the truth that the things of nature are nothing more than ideas directly communicated to us by God, enables us to develop an almost immediate awareness or "seeing" of God's presence in nature. Instead of seeing all things in God, we come to see *God's creative and conserving presence* in all the sensible things of our perception. The ideas imparted to us constitute a rational discourse, testifying to the intelligence, power, and benevolence of the infinite spirit. The world of bodily phenomena can be viewed in two ways: by sense and by intellect.[39] *By sense* and the scientific disciplines, nature is considered immanently, for its own sake. With the aid of the pure *intellect,* however, philosophy considers nature precisely as God's effect, proposed to man's mind. From this perspective, the world of sensible things is a region of fleeting shadows, adumbrating the intelligible world of spirits. Only mind, in its intellectual function, can grasp the sensible and intelligible orders together, as aspects of a single, interrelated universe. Just as notions are required in order to know the reality of minds and their operations, so notions are the proper means for apprehending the *relations* that bind different natures — things of sense and persons — together in the unity of existence.

One of Berkeley's earliest annotations was that "nothing properly

[38] On nature as God's language, cf. *An Essay towards a New Theory of Vision,* 147, 152 *(Works,* I, 231, 233); *The Principles of Human Knowledge,* I, 44, 108 *(Works,* II, 59, 88: *ad lin.* 25); *Alciphron,* IV, 6–7, 11–15 *(Works,* III, 148–149, 155–162).

[39] The dualism of sense and intellect is quite pronounced in *Siris,* 293–295, 348–349 *(Works,* V, 136–137, 157).

but persons, i.e., conscious things, do exist: all other things are not so much existences as manners [*in the later works:* objects] of the existence of persons."[40] This intensely *personalistic* view of the universe of beings underlies his entire doctrine on minds and their objects; in the *Siris,* it is combined with a theory of *participation in being.* One of the abiding difficulties in Berkeley's system is the metaphysical status of finite minds. They are described as *active* beings, in contradistinction to ideas. Yet they are equally effects of the infinite power, and therefore have a *receptive* side. They obtain their substantial reality and their ideas of sense from God. Berkeley never effects a complete reconciliation of the active and receptive aspects, but a step toward a solution is taken in his notion of participation, which he derived from his readings in Plotinus, Proclus, and other Neo-Platonists. Like his American counterpart, Jonathan Edwards, he underlines the participated character of all finite minds. A finite person exists, not only by perceiving ideas, but primarily by receiving these ideas precisely as gifts, coming from the unity of the infinite person. The personal self stands in just as much need of its ideas or objects of perception as the latter stand in need of the self. But the mind attains a fully personal grasp upon itself, only when it realizes that its *need for ideas* is only a phase in its *greater need for the divine source* of all ideas and minds. Hence the receptivity of the human mind is not an utterly passive and inert condition, such as that of the ideas. The human mind can reflectively recognize the source of its ideas, and so can elevate itself, by a free response of gratitude and worship, to the wholly active being of God.

Human persons are neither wholly passive, like ideas, nor wholly active, like God. They stand in a midway position, and can share in both extremes. Personal reality is constituted precisely by the mind, inasmuch as it participates intelligently and willingly in the unity and being of the divine mind. This sharing of personal reality, in and through God, leads to a communion of individual human spirits. Leibniz and Berkeley come by diverse routes to much the same final view of the *City of God,* as a unity of uncreated spirit and created spirits, in which God Himself is the bond of personal being among them.

[40] *Philosophical Commentaries,* 24 (*Works,* I, 10; spelling and punctuation modernized); cf. *Siris,* 346–347 (*Works,* V, 156–157). Residual difficulties are discussed by J. A. Mourant, "Some Unresolved Issues in Berkeley's Natural Theology," *Philosophical Studies,* 15 (1966), 58–75.

SUMMARY

Berkeley's ultimate purpose of moral and religious reform motivated his denial of matter, i.e., of a substance supposed to be unknowable and yet to exist independently of any mind, divine or human. Matter can be removed, without making any difference in either the scientific or the common-sense outlooks, and hence without leading to general skepticism. The general meaning of ideas can be explained satisfactorily in terms of particular ideas and their relations, without recourse to abstraction proper or to abstract general ideas. Above all, a coherent immaterialist exegesis of common-sense convictions can be made. Berkeley did not turn to untutored common sense but rather to Locke's description of the understanding. What more does the Lockean individual mean by a sensible thing, Berkeley inquired, than that which is perceived, precisely *qua* perceived? Now, that which is perceived as such is only an idea. An idea cannot be present in an unperceiving substance, such as matter. Nor can anything resembling an idea be present in an unperceiving, material subject, since an idea can be like only another idea. There are only two general modes of existence: perceiving and being perceived, minds and sensible things or ideas. Neither solipsism nor chaotic subjectivism need follow from this immaterialist New Principle, according to Berkeley's explanation. He used the passive character of ideas of sense to prove the existence of God as their first cause and the cause of one's own spiritual being, as a mind. There are also positive signs indicating the presence of other finite minds, although Berkeley was unable to offer more than probable arguments for their existence. God communicates ideas or sensible things to our minds in a stable, predictable way, thus providing a basis for scientific laws (which are, however, noncausal in character). Like Leibniz, Berkeley looked to God as the common bond among minds or spirits. Finite persons can participate in the spiritual perfections of God, and thus join together in a community of perceiving and willing operations.

BIBLIOGRAPHICAL NOTE

1. *Sources.* All scholarly references are now made to the critical edition: *The Works of George Berkeley, Bishop of Cloyne* (9 Vols., London: Nelson, 1948–1957), ed. by A. A. Luce and T. E. Jessop. This includes Berkeley's correspondence and important letters addressed to him. It is noteworthy that the *Philosophical Commentaries,* edited by Luce (in Vol. I of the Luce-Jessop ed.) definitively replaces the editions of the so-called "Commonplace Book" offered by A. C. Fraser in Vol. I of his older edition of Berkeley (Oxford: Clarendon, 1901), and by G. A. Johnston, *Berkeley's Commonplace Book* (London: Faber and Faber, 1930). Berkeley's main treatises are reprinted for student use in several collections, including: *Berkeley Selections* (New York: Scribner, 1929), ed. by M. W. Calkins; *Philosophical Writings* (Austin: University of Texas Press, 1953),

ed. by T. E. Jessop; *Berkeley's Philosophical Writings* (New York: Macmillan, 1965), ed. by D. M. Armstrong; *Principles, Dialogues, and Philosophical Correspondence* (Indianapolis: Bobbs-Merrill, 1965), ed. by C. M. Turbayne; *Works on Vision* (Indianapolis: Bobbs-Merrill, 1963), ed. by C. M. Turbayne.

2. *Studies.* A. A. Luce, himself an enthusiastic Berkeleyan, has written the definitive biography, *The Life of George Berkeley, Bishop of Cloyne* (London: Nelson, 1949). We are indebted to A. A. Luce for three other important studies in the Berkeleyan field: *The Dialectic of Immaterialism* (London: Hodder and Stoughton, 1963), tracing the genesis of Berkeley's philosophy; *Berkeley's Immaterialism: A Commentary on his "Treatise concerning the Principles of Human Knowledge"* (London: Nelson, 1945), an incisive analysis of the *Principles;* and the comparative study, *Berkeley and Malebranche: A Study in the Origins of Berkeley's Thought* (New York: Oxford University Press, 1934). Other useful introductory books are: G. D. Hicks, *Berkeley* (London: Benn, 1932); G. J. Warnock, *Berkeley* (Baltimore: Penguin Books, 1953), showing Berkeley's attractiveness for analytic thinkers; and A. L. Leroy, *George Berkeley* (Paris: Presses Universitaires, 1959), which compares him with other British and French philosophers. J. O. Wisdom's *The Unconscious Origins of Berkeley's Philosophy* (New York: Hillary House, 1957) is a rather wild psychoanalytic interpretation of his immaterialist outlook.

The bearing of Berkeley's early research upon his mature epistemology is brought out by D. M. Armstrong, *Berkeley's Theory of Vision* (Melbourne: Melbourne University Press, 1960). That Berkeley is engaged in undermining the Cartesian-Newtonian metaphor and metaphysics of mechanism by the substitution of the metaphor of vision as a divine-human language, is the theme of C. M. Turbayne's *The Myth of Metaphor* (New Haven: Yale University Press, 1962). Whereas Luce regards the doctrinal position of the *Principles* as subsequently unchanged, the case for internal development of thought is made by: G. A. Johnston, *The Development of Berkeley's Philosophy* (New York: Macmillan, 1923); J. Wild, *George Berkeley: A Study of His Life and Philosophy* (Cambridge: Harvard University Press, 1936), with emphasis on the sermons and later religious orientation; F. Bender, *George Berkeley's Philosophy Re-examined* (Amsterdam: H. Paris, 1946), arguing for a strain of rationalistic idealism in the *Siris.* Berkeley's approach to God and religion is examined from different perspectives by: E. A. Sillem, *George Berkeley and the Proofs for the Existence of God* (London: Longmans, Green, 1957); M. Guéroult, *Berkeley: Quatres études sur la perception et sur Dieu* (Paris: Aubier, 1956); I. Hedenius, *Sensationalism and Theology in Berkeley's Philosophy* (Uppsala, Almqvist and Wiksell, 1936); N. Baladi, *La Pensée religieuse de Berkeley et l'unité de sa philosophie* (Paris: Vrin, 1945).

The early criticism of Berkeley's philosophy is investigated by H. M. Bracken, *The Early Reception of Berkeley's Immaterialism, 1710–1733* 2 ed. (The Hague: Nijhoff, 1965). His trip to America is described by B. Rand, *Berkeley's American Sojourn* (Cambridge: Harvard University

Press, 1932). One may consult J. L. Blau, *Men and Movements in American Philosophy* (New York: Prentice-Hall, 1952), pp. 12–27, on Jonathan Edwards and Samuel Johnson. Evidence of Berkeley's continuing relevance for contemporary philosophy is afforded by two collective volumes: *George Berkeley* (*University of California Publications in Philosophy*, Vol. 29, 1957), and *New Studies in Berkeley's Philosophy* (New York: Holt, Rinehart, 1966), ed. by W. E. Steinkraus.

Chapter III. DAVID HUME

I. LIFE AND WRITINGS

DAVID HUME (born, 1711, in Edinburgh) was the younger son
of the laird of Ninewells, who died when David was a baby. He was
educated at Ninewells by his mother and then at Edinburgh College
(c. 1721-1725). The Arts course consisted of Greek, logic, metaphysics,
and Newtonian natural philosophy, with options in ethics and history.
Although he tried to study law and then to enter commerce, his
heart was fixed upon religious and philosophical problems. Finally,
he resolved to retire to France (1734), where he did private studies
at Reims and then at La Flèche. Hume was certainly conversant with
the writings of Locke, Berkeley, Hutcheson, Malebranche, and Bayle,
but his reticence about his readings makes it difficult to trace his
sources. Before coming to London in 1737, he had already finished
his major work, *A Treatise of Human Nature*. The first two volumes
were published in 1739 and the third in 1740. Although Hume re-
ported that this anonymously issued book "fell dead-born from the
press," it did receive a long but not very enlightened review. But
through the offices of Francis Hutcheson, who held the chair of moral
philosophy at Glasgow, the *Treatise* was brought to the attention of
Adam Smith, then a student at Glasgow. Hume's friendship with
Smith was lifelong. In order to gain the wide audience he desired,
Hume next sent to the printer the more popular *Essays Moral and
Political* (1741-1742), which sold very well. The success of this book
convinced Hume that he should revise the *Treatise* in more polished
style, making the argument more concise and orderly, and thus
emphasizing its central themes. In the meanwhile, however, he made
an unsuccessful bid (1745) for the chair of "ethics and pneumatic
philosophy," at the University of Edinburgh. His reputation as a
skeptic and atheist stood in the way of this appointment. Hume
quickly compensated for this setback by obtaining a post as secretary

to General St Clair, accompanying him first on an ill-fated expedition against the French and then on a diplomatic mission to Vienna and Turin.

While he was on the diplomatic mission, Hume's revision of the first part of the *Treatise* appeared as *Philosophical Essays concerning Human Understanding* (1748). This book, later known as *An Enquiry concerning Human Understanding,* high-lighted the problems of causality and skepticism and added two chapters on miracles, providence, and immortality. Returning to Ninewells in 1749, Hume spent three years upon an intensive writing project. His *An Enquiry concerning the Principles of Morals* (1751) went over the same ground as Book Three of the *Treatise;* his *Political Discourses* (1752) dealt with subjects of common interest and increased his renown both at home and abroad; his *Dialogues concerning Natural Religion* (withheld from publication until 1779) set forth his mind upon the problem of God's existence and the nature of religion. When his brother married (1751), Hume and his sister moved permanently to Edinburgh, where at last he received an official appointment as Keeper of the Advocates' Library (1752; resigned, 1757). Since this office gave him access to a vast collection of books, Hume undertook to write the history of England. The four volumes which he completed (1754–1761) became a focal point of contemporary controversy between Whigs and Tories. He also found time to edit *Four Dissertations* (1757), which dealt with the passions (his restatement of Book Two of the *Treatise*), tragedy, taste, and the natural history of religion. In the process of winnowing his materials, Hume destroyed an essay on geometry, at the advice of a mathematician, and left for posthumous publication his *Two Essays on Suicide and Immortality* (1777), which his friends deemed too outspoken for safety. Thereafter, Hume wrote nothing of great consequence.

But his fame had increased considerably and, at its height, he was invited to serve as acting secretary to the British embassy in Paris (1763). At the latter capitol, "le bon David" was lionized by the ladies and eagerly sought after by intellectuals like Helvétius, D'Alembert, Buffon, Turgot, Holbach, and Diderot. Hume thoroughly enjoyed the green fields of amusement but did not allow the adulation to turn his head. In 1766, he returned to London with Rousseau, in order to provide the latter with a quiet and secure abode. Rousseau's habitual egoism and suspicion led to the inevitable break and public quarrel. Hume stayed in London for a while as Undersecretary of

State (in charge of ecclesiastical patronage in Scotland!) and retired at last to Edinburgh in 1769, with an adequate income. He built a town house on St. David Street, entertained his friends at dinner, and shocked the troubled Boswell, when the latter questioned him about a future life. Hume summed up his character in a brief autobiographical sketch and died in 1776, after insuring in his will the publication of his *Dialogues concerning Natural Religion*.

2. THE TRUE SKEPTIC AND THE SCIENCE OF HUMAN NATURE

Like everyone else, Hume had his moments of dogmatic certainty and also his moments of skeptical doubt. Both his temperament and his philosophy were compounded of these two moods. He oscillated between belief and doubt, looking always for a means of synthesizing them and often playing the one against the other. In the privacy of his chamber, his intense speculation would tear down the fabric of certainty and common conviction. Then, he would surrender himself to the amenities of social life, playing at backgammon and meeting practical situations as they arose. In retrospect, his speculative doubts would seem to be artificial and overstated; yet honesty and an inquiring spirit would invariably send him back to the same meditations. From such experiences, he learned that the only balance open to him was to maintain an *equal diffidence* before both his philosophical doubts and his practical convictions. His motto was: "Be a philosopher; but, amidst all your philosophy, be still a man."[1] This rule enabled him to carry his speculations to the extreme, without losing the facility to enjoy the natural reliefs of social intercourse, business, and downright self-forgetfulness.

A distinction must be drawn, however, between two sorts of *dogmatism,* only one of which Hume was ready to defend. There is need for steady working beliefs, as a support to *practical* decisions. But it is the common error of most minds to confuse this exigency, at the pragmatic level, with a host of uncritical convictions of a *speculative* sort. Against this "metaphysical" dogmatism of both

[1] *An Enquiry concerning Human Understanding,* I (edited by Selby-Bigge, 9); cf. *ibid.,* Section XII: "Of the Academical or Sceptical Philosophy" (Selby-Bigge, 149–165). On the nature of Hume's skepticism, cf. P. Stanley, "The Scepticisms of David Hume," *The Journal of Philosophy,* 32 (1935), 421–431, and R. H. Popkin, "David Hume: His Pyrrhonism and His Critique of Pyrrhonism," *The Philosophical Quarterly,* I (1950–1951), 385–407. Also, J. V. McGlynn, "The Two Skepticisms in Hume's Treatise," *The Thomist,* 20 (1957), 419–446.

ordinary people and his philosophical predecessors, Hume found the skeptical attitude a useful antidote. He distinguished, however, between antecedent and consequent skepticism. *Antecedent skepticism* is represented by the Cartesian methodic doubt. Hume did not think that any man could sincerely embrace this outlook, in all its force. Even if it could be done, its only value would be the negative one of clearing out old prejudices and misconceptions. Methodic doubt is not a constructive method in philosophy, since it rests on the false assumption that some privileged principle can resist doubt. The net effect of the British empiricist movement and Malebranche's philosophy was, in Hume's eyes, to discredit forever the Cartesian conception of the substantial, thinking self, as the starting point in philosophy. And it is impossible to take a single forward step, unless one is prepared to use the very faculties which methodic doubt is supposed to call in question.

There remains the *consequent* type of *skepticism,* which does not start with a general doubt but which is the outcome of detailed inquiries into the actual exercise of our mind. Hume knew and employed the familiar arguments of Sextus Empiricus, as brought up to date in Bayle's *Dictionary*. But he did not think that the skeptical arguments against the *senses,* based on sensory illusions and deceptions, went deeply enough. They only proved that the senses, by themselves, are insufficient for gaining truth. They still left open the possibility that certainty lies within our grasp, provided that *reason* be invoked and that one make allowance for the condition of the medium and organs of sensation. Far more radical were the implications of Berkeley's empirical criticism of primary qualities and an independent material world. For, this criticism bore upon the natural tendency of the mind to believe the testimony of the senses, even under optimum conditions. Furthermore, Berkeley's animadversions on abstract ideas, space, time, and mathematics brought reason itself within the pale of doubt. The outcome could well be complete Pyrrhonism, which is the suicide of all our knowing powers.

It might be necessary, Hume observed, to pass through the purgatory of *absolute, Pyrrhonian skepticism,* but one need not take up permanent residence there. For absolute skepticism renders one unfit for action as well as for speculation, so that it gives birth to no positive, durable good. Hume was moving toward a more moderate sort of consequent skepticism, which would continue the empiricist attack upon pure, abstract reason and yet find a basis for conduct.

He referred to his position as a *mitigated* or *true skepticism*. Its two outstanding features are a concentration of analysis upon the problems of man and an adaptation of the Newtonian method to achieve this purpose.

This dual aspect of Hume's program is well stated in the subtitle of *A Treatise of Human Nature:* "An Attempt to Introduce the Experimental Method of Reasoning into Moral Subjects." This is a vindication of Hobbes for stressing the investigation of human nature, and of Bacon for holding that the same method used in natural philosophy should also be applied to man. The proper perspective in philosophy is only acquired when the *study of human nature* is recognized as being central. The other sciences are somehow tributary to this study, and "instead of taking now and then a castle or village on the frontier, [the philosopher ought] to march directly to the capital or center of these sciences, to human nature itself."[2] This dependence is apparent in the more humane disciplines: logic, morals, esthetics, and politics. But it is present also in mathematics, natural philosophy, and natural religion (disciplines which deal with some object other than man), since their objects must be brought within the range of our minds and must be judged by our knowing powers. Hume uses the term *moral subjects* in a broad way, to include all philosophical investigations into the nature and limits of our understanding, passions, and sentiments, as well as the principles of belief in matters of fact and the principles of conduct.

Just as the other sciences depend upon the cardinal science of man, so the latter is constituted by an application of Newton's experimental philosophy to moral subjects. *Newton's rules of reasoning and method* find their psychological and ethical equivalents in statements made by Hume. The true skeptic must avoid any appeal to occult powers in nature or in the mind. He must avoid purely abstract and rationalistic hypotheses about the constitution of material and spiritual substances or about our reasoning ability. He should draw his evidence from experience and observation, refer all his proposition to their sensory origin, be parsimonious in his causal explanations, and proceed gradually to a few general principles governing all mental phenomena. Hume transfers from natural to humane philosophy the scientific proscription against claims to have knowledge of the essences

---

[2] *A Treatise of Human Nature,* Introduction (Selby-Bigge, xx).

of things.[3] Minds, no less than bodies, remain completely unknowable territory for the true skeptic, who seeks to develop an experimental philosophy of man. This *restriction of knowledge to the appearances* is taken by Hume as the distinguishing feature of the only "true metaphysics": the *phenomenalistic* study of human nature. This is significant, since Hume is thereby enabled, at the outset, to define experience in purely phenomenalistic terms and to rule out, as "going beyond experience," any efforts to ascertain substantial essences or ultimate principles of being. His decision to introduce the Newtonian method into philosophical anthropology is not a purely methodological one but is laden down with epistemological and metaphysical consequences for the interpretation of experience.

The limitation of our understanding to appearances is no more a reason for discouragement in the science of man than in the other sciences. Once we become reconciled to foregoing any ultimate ontological principles, we are free to observe the uniformities within our experience, identify and demarcate the powers at work, and render our principles of explanation as general as possible within empirical bounds. Yet Hume sees an important difference between experimental procedures in natural and in moral philosophy. The natural sciences can make deliberate experiments with bodies, without affecting the results in any way. (This assertion was legitimate in classical modern physics, where the problem of the influence of our measuring operations upon the data was not acute.) But in moral philosophy, the reflective deliberation with which we collect the evidence, is apt to disturb the natural operation of our mental principles. The science

---

[3] "To me it seems evident, that the essence of the mind being equally unknowable to us with that of external bodies, it must be equally impossible to form any notion of its qualities and powers otherwise than from careful and exact experiments, and the observation of those particular effects, which result from its different circumstances and situations. And though we must endeavour to render all our principles as uniform as possible, by tracing up our experiments to the utmost, and explaining all effects from the simplest and fewest causes, it is still certain we cannot go beyond experience; and any hypothesis that pretends to discover the ultimate original qualities of human nature, ought at first [i.e., at once] to be rejected as presumptuous and chimerical. . . . As long as we confine our speculations to *the appearances* of objects to our sense, without entering into disquisitions concerning their real nature and operations, we are safe from all difficulties." *Ibid.*, Introduction and Appendix (Selby-Bigge, xxi, 638; spelling modernized here and throughout this chapter). Thus from first to last, the *Treatise* assumes that the methodological and epistemological limitations of Newtonian mechanics, skepticism, and phenomenalism must be imposed upon philosophy as a whole.

of man is the one discipline where the *investigator* also becomes an
object of study; it is the one science where *introspection* may operate
to gather direct evidence about the questions at issue. Although aware
of this new situation, Hume does not appreciate the far-reaching
methodological changes that are entailed by these basic contrasts
between the study of man and the study of the rest of nature. It was
left for Kant to remark that, however much we would like a strict
parallel to obtain between physical and mental operations, the Newtonian method is transferred to man only by way of a certain
— "analogy" and on the strength of faith in that "analogy." In any
case, the comparison is too loose to sustain the inference that philosophy of man must confine itself to a description of appearances.

3. THE ELEMENTS OF HUMAN COGNITION

True to his chosen method, Hume begins with an analytic reduction
of our cognitive operations. He subscribes unquestioningly to the
elementaristic view of Locke and Berkeley: that our knowledge and
belief are best understood, when they are broken down into their elements, evaluated in terms of these constituents, and reconstructed
from the analytic units. In the most general sense, the contents of
experience are *perceptions*.[4] Hume proposes "perceptions" rather than
Locke's "ideas," as the broadest descriptive term for mental contents,
since he wants to stress the derived and referential nature of our
ideas. The fundamental division of perceptions is into *impressions*
and *ideas*. The former strike our mind with great force and vivacity,
whereas the latter are relatively weak and languid. The impressions
include all our sensations, passions, and emotions, considered precisely in their first, lively appearance to the mind. There is no difference in kind between impressions and ideas, since the greater or lesser
force of perceptions concerns only the manner and degree in which
they strike the mind. The ideas are derived from the impressions.
Hume assumes that because ideas are *derivatives*, they must also be
copies or faint images of the impressions. But Locke had maintained
that the ideas of secondary qualities are derived from bare objective
powers or qualities and yet do not resemble these powers.

---

[4] *Ibid.*, I, i, 1 (Selby-Bigge, 1–7); *An Enquiry concerning Human Understanding*, II
(Selby-Bigge, 18–22).

Hume on the Elements of Cognition

Perceptions	Impressions	of sensation of reflection	Simple and complex
	Ideas	of memory of imagination	

Hume encounters some difficulty in defending the *distinction* between impressions and ideas. First of all, he appeals to our common-sense recognition of the difference between seeing something (having an impression) and thinking about what one has seen (having an idea). This corresponds roughly to Berkeley's distinction between having ideas of sense and having ideas of imagination. But Hume is more willing than Berkeley to admit that the distinction breaks down in some particular instances, whereas so many metaphysical implications flow from Berkeley's contrast that he rigidly retains it in all cases. The criterion of force and liveliness fails, for instance, to cover situations in which our impressions are so low in intensity that they cannot be distinguished from "weak images." And in sleep, fever, or madness, ideas may be entertained with a degree of conviction and vividness that surpasses the force of most impressions. Under normal conditions, however, at least the *derived* and *referential* character of ideas sets them off from impressions. In some way, ideas come from impressions and point back to them. On the contrary, there is a self-contained quality about impressions which makes them the original perceptions of the mind.

Hume warns against basing a verbal argument upon the word "impressions." This term does not signify the manner of *production* of our original perceptions, but only the manner of their *entertainment* by the mind, and hence the inference cannot be made that they are imprinted on the mind by some external cause. Despite this protest, however, Hume's own usage often suggests such an inference. For he refers to the senses as inlets of perception, as well as to the secret, unknowable causes in nature that affect our organic states. Like Locke and Berkeley, he maintains and profits by an undeclared relationship between phenomenalism and common-sense realism.

In order to throw further light on the relations among perceptions, Hume makes a division between simple and complex impressions, and between simple and complex ideas. *Simple* perceptions, whether impressions or ideas, admit of no further separation into parts: they

are the terminations of analysis in their own order. *Complex* perceptions, whether impressions or ideas, do permit further analysis and
decomposition into constituent parts. This distinction helps to correct
the preliminary view that there is a perfect correspondence between
all impressions and all ideas. Clearly enough, there may be a complex
idea, such as "The New Jerusalem," for which there is no corresponding complex impression. Conversely, to the complex impression a man
on a parapet gains of the city of Paris, there is no complex idea that
adequately reproduces its original in every detail. Despite the rough
resemblance of our complex ideas to our complex impressions, the
former are not always exact and exhaustive copies of the latter.

Nevertheless, Hume ventures the general proposition that at least
"every simple idea has a simple impression, which resembles it; and
every simple impression a correspondent idea."[5] This minimal position
must be maintained at all costs. Otherwise, metaphysical statements
cannot be criticized, by appeal to the *empirical criterion* of tracing
back ideas to their corresponding impressions or empirical sources.
The Humean conception of experience cannot be made the measure
of all knowledge and belief, unless this *relation of origin* obtains,
along with the implication that correspondence entails an exact *resemblance* between simple impressions and ideas. Despite the burden
placed upon the proposition, Hume admits at least one exception,
which Descartes and others had already pointed out. When the mind
considers a series of colors arranged in a graduated scale, it is able to
interpolate the idea or image of a shade not previously encountered in
experience. Hume regards this phenomenon as too restricted in nature
to merit closer examination or to require any drastic revision of his
theory about simple impressions and ideas. Nevertheless, this exception does weaken the universality of the empirical criterion and
opens up the possibility that other simple ideas (not necessarily
limited to color qualities) may have an independent origin, due to
the mind's constructive activity, and yet may also be valid for
experience.

Our impressions, whether simple or complex, can be subdivided into
those of sensation and those of reflection.[6] *Impressions of sensation*
are due to unknown causes and must simply be accepted as original

[5] *A Treatise of Human Nature,* I, i, 1 (Selby-Bigge, 3). For an analysis of Hume's
difficulties in respect to this proposition, read C. Maund, "Hume's Treatment of
Simples," *Proceedings of the Aristotelian Society,* N.S., 35 (1934–1935), 209–228.
[6] *A Treatise of Human Nature,* I, i, 2 (Selby-Bigge, 7–8).

factors of perception. The empiricist limitation of the mind to its own perceptions erects a barrier against any philosophical study of these causes. Like Locke, Hume leaves such investigations to the physicists and anatomists, without inquiring too closely into the scientific status of their findings. He is chiefly interested in the *impressions of reflection,* which include desires, passions, and emotions, along with certain determinations of the mind that are relevant to the question of belief and causal judgments. This second type of impression does not derive from unknown causes but can definitely be traced to our ideas. After the sensation of some pleasure or pain, for instance, there remains an idea of this pleasure or pain. When the idea is recalled by memory or imagination, it will produce a new impression of desire or aversion: this new emotional state is an impression of reflection. It presupposes the impression of sensation and the idea that arouses the reflection.

This explanation obliges Hume to admit that *temporal priority* and *underived originality* do not absolutely differentiate all impressions from all ideas. Impressions of reflection are subsequent to, and derived from, certain ideas. In view of the admitted exceptions to Hume's proposed criteria of liveliness, force, temporal priority, and underived originality, the only unyielding mark definitively setting off impressions from ideas is the nonreferential nature of impressions, as contrasted with the representative nature of ideas. However, this mark is a matter of *stipulated definition* with Hume, for otherwise the empiricist criterion would have no firm basis. This definition is an extra-empirical factor at the heart of Hume's method.

Hume concludes his survey of the elements of cognition with a distinction between ideas (simple or complex) of *memory* and *imagination.* He gives a descriptive account of the "faculties" of memory and imagination, without making any metaphysical commitment in their favor. He offers two ways of distinguishing between their operation. Once present in the mind, impressions may reappear as ideas, which have either retained some of their original vivacity or have lost it. An idea of memory is one that enjoys a vivacity intermediate between the impression itself and a mere idea of imagination. The latter is faint and unsteady, having lost the original force and liveliness. Yet Hume himself points out the defect in this first manner of distinction, since memories may often be weaker than images of a vivid imagination. Hence, as a second basis of distinction, he suggests that memory is tied down by the order and form of the original impressions, whereas imagination is free in these respects. But even

the office of memory, reproducing the order and position of the
original impressions, does not give it a privileged epistemological
status, since its operations can never be checked against an independent record — which would itself be an instance of memory. The
prospects for an empirical theory of knowledge and belief depend,
perforce, upon the successful establishment of a connection between
imagination and reality.

4. IMAGINATION AND THE ASSOCIATION OF IDEAS

The gravamen of Hume's mitigated skepticism is located in his
theory of the imagination, which seems to be at once the most chaotic
and the most harmonious power of the mind. Imagination not only
reproduces the mere ideas or pale images but is also able to transpose
and fuse them in an untrammeled way. Hume's originality lies, not
in repeating this venerable distinction between reproductive and
productive imagination, but in combining it with his *main logical
doctrine*. That doctrine is stated as follows:

> Whatever is distinct, is distinguishable; and whatever is distinguish-
> able, is separable by the thought or imagination. All perceptions are
> distinct. They are, therefore, distinguishable, and separable, and may
> be conceived as separately existent, and may exist separately, without
> any contradiction or absurdity.[7]

Imagination could not compose winged steeds and other fancies, were
it not able to decompose complex ideas into their simple components
and to detach one simple idea from another. Because ideas are copies
of impressions, they must submit to the conditions imposed by impressions. All simple impressions are distinct, self-contained, atomic
units, which are separable from each other. Therefore, all simple ideas
are likewise distinct and separable, imagination being the keen-edged
sword that cleaves one simple idea from another and assigns it freely
to another partner. Taken objectively by themselves, our simple ideas

---

[7] *Ibid.*, Appendix (Selby-Bigge, 634). This principle is the ground for Hume's
view that the objects of experience are loose and unconnected, and that therefore
the source of the causal belief must be a subjective one. M. C. Beardsley, "A Dilemma for
Hume," *The Philosophical Review*, 42 (1943), 28–46, suggests that the doctrine
of the looseness of the factors in experience holds true only of "objects" or the
analytic elements, isolated for purposes of intrinsic description alone. But it does not
give an accurate account of the actual "events," which furnish the materials and basis
for analysis, since our experience of actual "events" manifests irreducible connections
and references of a contextual sort, which Hume's logical principle fails to respect.
The same conclusion is reached by Charles Hartshorne, "Hume's Metaphysics and Its
Present-Day Influence," *The New Scholasticism*, 35 (1961), 152–171.

are *loose* and *unconnected,* providing imagination with plastic materials for its own synthetic operations.

It is not unexpected to find Hume affirming also that what imagination conceives separately, may also be conceived as existing separately and may, indeed, exist separately. This is the rationalistic side of empiricism, carried through to the extreme point where the *possibilities of imagination* are also the *possibilities of existence*. Since the only realities attainable in experience are perceptual objects (i.e., perceptions *as* objects), every idea that is separately imaginable has at least a *logically* irrefutable claim to existence. Hume can discover no character of existence over and above the determinate content of the object or idea itself. *Existence* is not an additional predicate but is simply the *idea grasped as a perception or distinct object*. "Whatever we conceive, we conceive to be existent."[8] As far as logically necessary grounds of argument are concerned, there is no reason against supposing that whatever can be conceived separately by imagination, can also exist as a distinct entity.

But were this all that could be said, ours would be a nightmare world of arbitrary constructions of imagination. Since this is not actually the case, Hume concludes that our familiar experience cannot be explained satisfactorily by an analysis that concentrates exclusively upon the ideas as isolated objects or meaning-contents. There are *real, coherent wholes* of experience that never become confused with products of our free fancy. Instead of looking beyond imagination, to an *intellectual* power that could grasp the unity and existential act of things, however, Hume prefers to account for our coherent grasp of realities in terms of *imagination* itself — the very power which seems to reduce everything to arbitrary combinations. This is a bold stroke. But in order to invoke imagination in this new role, he must strengthen it with the operations of the so-called laws of association.

As Hobbes and Malebranche had already noted, the imagination is not a completely erratic and lawless power. It exhibits some well-defined constants, that lead it to combine ideas in definite ways. But it does not make its combinations *in virtue of necessary, objective connections* discovered among the ideas themselves. For, from the objective standpoint of the ideas, everything is loose and *un*connected: the bonds established by imagination are not based on the logical implications or internal relations among ideas. Hume turns

[8] *A Treatise of Human Nature,* I, ii, 6 (Selby-Bigge, 67).

to "nature," i.e., to the forces secretly at work on the *subjective* side of the mind. The *gentle force of association* inclines the imagination to make connections which, although not strictly inseparable, are often uniform and enduring, so that one idea naturally tends to introduce another in the mind. What the precise nature of this mental principle may be, Hume professes to remain ignorant. It is a kind of universal attraction, doing for the mental world what Newton's force of gravity does for the physical world. Just as Newton was able to calculate the effects of gravity, without ever perceiving its essence, so Hume is content to chart the course and consequences of the associative force, without inquiring into its ultimate foundation. In his philosophy, it remains an *unanalyzed given factor,* whose origin and structure are shrouded in the mystery of what he himself calls, in another context, "that vague undeterminate word *nature.*"[9]

Hume speaks enthusiastically about the *three principles of association:* resemblance, contiguity in time or place, and cause-and-effect. He hails them both as constituting the "universal principle, which had an equal influence on all mankind" and as supplying *"to us* the cement of the universe."[10] It must be assumed that they are found uniformly among all men, for otherwise no inference could be made from their operation in one individual's experience to the common conditions of human nature. Furthermore, they are needed as cement, in the sense of saving empiricism from the atomistic consequences of the analysis of ideas and existence. Whereas Locke appeals to perception, and Berkeley to God's continuous providence, Hume looks to imagination and the principles of association for a counteragent to the analytic emphasis upon ideas as elements. If ideas are naturally attracted together by a certain force operating upon imagination, then experience will consist of a connected series of images, joined in coherent wholes, rather than of an antic dance of detached fancies. Judgment is the perception of such connections.

On one capital point, however, Hume admits that the forces of mental attraction differ from those of physical attraction. The principles of mental association are the only *general* ones to provide

---

[9] *Dialogues concerning Natural Religion,* VII (edited by Smith, 178; italics mine); cf. *An Enquiry concerning the Principles of Morals,* Appendix III (Selby-Bigge, 307).

[10] *An Enquiry concerning Human Understanding,* III (Selby-Bigge, 23); *An Abstract of a Treatise of Human Nature* (edited by J. M. Keynes and P. Sraffa, 32). See also, *A Treatise of Human Nature,* I, i, 4 (Selby-Bigge, 10–13). J. K. Ryan has worked out the comparison with St. Thomas: "Aquinas and Hume on the Laws of Association," *The New Scholasticism,* 12 (1938), 366–377.

connections among ideas, but they are neither the *infallible* nor the *sole* causes of such connections. They act as a persuasive force upon imagination. Yet, unlike physical agents, imagination retains its intrinsic freedom and may be moved by other considerations to join ideas in unexpected ways. In addition, Hume follows the Newtonian popularizers, rather than Newton himself, in attributing *real, causal efficacy* to the universal force of attraction. These serious differences render questionable his arguments based on a comparison of mental association with gravity, and indicate clearly the obstacles against using the Newtonian method to construct a philosophy of human nature.

Three applications of Hume's doctrine of association are noteworthy. They concern: general ideas, the belief in reality, and causal connections.

In dealing with *abstract, general ideas,* Hume seems to be following Berkeley but, in fact, he comes closer to Hobbes' position. An abstract idea is one that is particular in its own nature, but general in its representation.[11] It acquires generality not from containing a universal *meaning* but from its connection with a general *term*. A term is called general in virtue of a twofold association that is built up in the mind *by usage:* first, between the term and the habit of the mind that evokes a particular idea; second, between the evoked idea and the other particular ideas with which customary bonds have been established. Upon presentation of the term, imagination not only calls forth the particular idea, associated with the term, but also places itself in a state of readiness to recall the remaining ideas in the associative group. The generality of abstract ideas resides in this readiness for associative recall of images in a family relation.

A second application of association is in explaining our *belief in reality*.[12] Taken in isolation from the associative force, imagination can never arouse a belief in the reality of its objects. For, taken in this way, it is merely exercising the privilege of separating and recombining, at will, perceptions that are intrinsically distinct and unconnected. We

---

[11] *A Treatise of Human Nature,* I, i, 7 (Selby-Bigge, 17–24). An extensive study of this question is made by R. I. Aaron, "Hume's Theory of Universals," *Proceedings of the Aristotelian Society,* N.S., 42 (1941–1942), 117–140, and (much more critically) by K. B. Price, "Hume's Analysis of Generality," *The Philosophical Review,* 59 (1950), 58–76. Price notes that Hume fails to provide any empirical objection against objectively repeatable qualities and relations, which could serve as the basis for universals, apart from the associative mechanism.

[12] On "reality" as a coherent system of beliefs, cf. *A Treatise of Human Nature,* I, iii, 9, and Appendix (Selby-Bigge, 108, 629).

accept the workings of imagination as real and existentially credible, only when they are guided systematically by the principles of association. It is only then that these operations approximate, in constancy and coherence, to the impressions of sensation. Apart from its bare beginnings in the impressions of sensation, the major portion of what Hume regards as belief in the real world is *a system of constant and coherent images,* knitted together by imagination, acting under the gentle promptings of the power of association. Berkeley's rigid criterion for determining real, sensible things is thus dissolved, giving Hume a thoroughly phenomenalistic meaning for "the real world."

Finally, Hume makes an innovation by including *cause-and-effect* among the aspects from which the association of ideas springs. In so doing, he is gradually formulating the problem of causality in a special way. For, the principles of association are brought to bear upon objects or ideas that do *not* have any intrinsic linkage, based on their own nature or operation. To reckon the bond of cause-and-effect among these principles is to suggest, at long range, that the objects themselves are somehow loose and unconnected, and that their causal union is due solely to a mental force generated by custom. This remote predetermination of the nature of the causal connection is advanced another step with Hume's discussion of relations, making his own solution of the causal problem a foregone conclusion.

5. RELATIONS AND REASONING

The association of ideas gives rise to the three Lockean classes of complex ideas: substances, modes, and relations. Hume makes short work of the general ideas of substance and mode. All of Berkeley's arguments against material substance tell against *substance as such.* Hume finds that the idea of substance can be traced to no distinctive impression, either of sense or of reflection. It owes its origin to a collection of simple ideas, united by imagination and given a common thing-name, which facilitates the recall of this particular collection. In the case of *mode,* the associative force is also needed to account for the unity of the complex idea. Hume proposes to extricate empiricism from the dead-end reached in previous analyses of substances and modes, by making a fresh start in the neglected area of relations. With him, the problem of relation comes to the forefront of empiricism, just as with Leibniz' discussion of harmony, it became centrally important for the rationalist school.

Hume's Theory of Relations

1. **Natural relations.**
   a) Resemblance.
   b) Contiguity in time or place. } Principles of association.
   c) Cause-and-effect.

2. **Philosophical relations.**

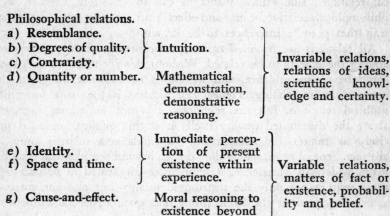

   a) Resemblance.
   b) Degrees of quality. } Intuition.
   c) Contrariety.
   d) Quantity or number. Mathematical demonstration, demonstrative reasoning.

   Invariable relations, relations of ideas, scientific knowledge and certainty.

   e) Identity.
   f) Space and time. } Immediate perception of present existence within experience.

   g) Cause-and-effect. Moral reasoning to existence beyond experience.

   Variable relations, matters of fact or existence, probability and belief.

(**N.B.** Compare: 1, a, b, c, with 2, a, f, g.)

A distinction is drawn between two main types of relation: natural and philosophical.[13] In *natural relations,* ideas are connected through the force of association, so that one introduces the other "naturally" or by customary reference. Hume regards this as the ordinary kind of relation meant when people say that certain things are related by a connecting principle. People mean that they experience a certain mental compulsion to turn their minds from one idea to the other. The natural relations are precisely those involved in association: resemblance, contiguity in time or place, and cause-and-effect. On the other hand, *philosophical relation* is simply any matter of comparison among objects, without implying any connecting principle or associative bond. Certain qualities of objects make them fit for mental comparison, so that we may make an *arbitrary* union of such objects

---

[13] *Ibid.,* I, i, 5; iii, 1–2 (Selby-Bigge, 13–15, 69–74).

or ideas (i.e., a union where there is no *natural* force, subjectively compelling the mind to refer from one term to the other). There are seven types of philosophical relation: resemblance, identity, space and time, quantity or number, degrees of quality, contrariety, cause-and-effect. It is noteworthy that resemblance, contiguity in space or time, and cause-and-effect may be viewed both as natural and as philosophical relations. But Hume wants to call in question whether, as a philosophical relation, cause-and-effect rests on any real, distinctive trait that permits inferences to be drawn.

All relations are founded upon some *common quality,* distributed among the objects to be related. Without this identical quality, there could be no resemblance, and without a resemblance no ground of comparison or relating. Hence, *resemblance* is the basis for philosophical relations. But the resemblance is not something over and above the distributed quality itself: it *is* this quality, regarded precisely as matter for comparison. Resemblance-as-such is only an abstract, general term, which does not go beyond the identical qualities given widely in experience. Resemblances implicated in natural relations require not only the distributed quality but also the force of association, leading the mind from one qualitative embodiment to another. Hume gives no definite indication, however, of how we know that there is an · *identical* quality that is only numerically multiplied.

Philosophical relations fall into the two wide subdivisions of invariable and variable relations. The *invariable relations* depend exclusively on the ideas under comparison: as long as the ideas remain the same, the relations also remain invariably the same. In conformity with the Cartesian and Lockean views of science, Hume states that only the invariable relations can provide *strict knowledge,* because of their *purely ideal* character. In this class, he includes the relations of resemblance, contrariety, degrees of quality, and proportions of quantity or number. The first three of these invariable or constant relations are discoverable at first sight, and hence belong to intuition rather than to demonstration. But the relations of quantity and number provide the matter for *mathematics,* which is therefore the only science constituted by strictly *demonstrative reasoning.* In the *Treatise,* Hume concedes perfect exactness and certainty only to arithmetic and algebra. Geometry does not attain perfect precision of measurement, since it concerns the general appearances of sense objects and is therefore limited by the variations and complexities of natural being. In the first *Enquiry,* however, he allows that pure geometry is also a demonstrative science, although he still rejects (along with Berkeley) an infinite divisibility of quantity, since this idea is at bottom particular and finitely determinate. Since Hume's main interest centers about metaphysical and moral problems, he does not provide any satisfactory, empirical account of the foundations of mathematics.

The *variable relations* are those of identity, time and place, and cause-and-effect. These relations may be changed, without entailing any change either in the objects so related or in their ideas. For instance, the relation of distance between two bodies may vary without variation in the objects (the complex impressions) or their corresponding ideas. Since these relations are not exclusively ideal, their establishment by the mind depends upon *experience* and *observation.* This involves a kind of reasoning or comparison of the objects entering into the relation. But Hume observes a difference between the comparisons that establish the inconstant relations of identity and of time and place, and the comparison at the basis of cause-and-effect. The former are not genuine reasonings at all but rather are *immediate perceptions,* since both the relata and the relation itself are presented to the senses for comparison. However, in trying to establish the causal relation, the mind must reason from a given object or impression to a cause or effect that is not given in experience. This inference is *sui generis.* It does not deal mathematically with ideal connections alone, for it concerns a variable rather than an invariable relation and seeks a bond among existents. Yet it does not find the relation given intuitively along with both terms of the relation, for it is a reasoning from what is given in experience to what is not so given.

The distinction between demonstrative and moral reasoning helps to demarcate the sphere of the causal inference. All reasoning consists in a discovery of the relations that objects bear to each other. These relations may be either *relations of ideas* or *matters of fact* (as Locke had already noted).[14] Hence there is a corresponding distinction between two kinds of reasoning: demonstrative and moral. *Demonstrative reasoning* investigates the relations between ideas. Here, the mind is concerned solely with its own defining operations and ideas, regardless of questions about actual existence. The proper objects of this abstract demonstration are relations of quantity and number.

---

[14] *An Enquiry concerning Human Understanding,* IV, 1 (Selby-Bigge, 25–26).

Hence only the mathematical sciences yield demonstrative knowledge, which Hume defines rationalistically as that sort of reasoning, a denial of whose conclusions entails a contradiction. Any attempt to extend the scope of demonstration beyond mathematical relations is bound to end in illusion. Matters of fact and existence can be investigated only by *moral reasoning*. The only *certitude* about existential affairs is gained, when sensation or memory immediately presents the objects in their relation. But memory never attains full certitude, because of the difficulties surrounding its verification.

Moral reasoning proper attempts to go beyond what is presented in sense perception and memory, in order to discover something about the existence or action of objects that lie beyond experience. The only relation upon which such reasoning can be founded is *cause-and-effect*. All "metaphysical" (in the pejorative sense of supraempirical) reasoning relies upon the appeal to causal relations. By this route, conclusions are reached concerning the existence of the external, substantial world, the human soul, and God. But such inferences concern matters of fact and must submit to the limitations placed upon moral reasoning. In the existential order, we can never hope to reach demonstrative knowledge. For a denial of an existential conclusion does not lead to any contradiction. In the realm of matters of fact, whatever *is,* may also *not be.* "The contrary of every matter of fact is still possible; because it can never imply a contradiction, and is conceived by the mind with the same facility and distinctness, as if ever so conformable to reality. . . . *Nothing we imagine is absolutely impossible.*"[15] Thus Hume invokes the Cartesian ideal of a demonstrative science and a criterion of clear and distinct ideas, which he identifies with vivid, sharp images. By comparison with this standard, one may never expect to gain more than probability through causal inference. Moral reasoning in general can never yield more than a high degree of *probability* or *moral certitude,* and causal reasoning can never surpass this intrinsic limitation.

Hume is now ready to explain the significance of regarding cause-and-effect now as a philosophical, and now as a natural, relation.[16] A *comparison of ideas* can be made with the aid of the philosophical relation of cause-and-effect, but an *actual connection among objects* can be made only by cause-and-effect considered as a natural relation.

---

15 *Ibid.* (Selby-Bigge, 25); *A Treatise of Human Nature,* I, ii, 2 (Selby-Bigge, 32).
16 *Ibid.,* I, iii, 6, 14 (Selby-Bigge, 92–94, 170).

As a philosophical relation, it depends upon resemblance. But it has been shown that philosophical resemblance is nothing more than the distribution of an identical quality among several *given* objects. This resemblance does not embrace the existence or qualities of objects not given in experience, so that there is no objective basis for extending the causal inference beyond experience. As a *philosophical* relation, in fact, cause-and-effect enjoys no independent status and makes no distinctive union of ideas. It is reducible to some variation of spatial or temporal relation, such as contiguity, succession of before-and-after, and constant togetherness. The philosophical relation of cause-and-effect supplies no foundation for metaphysical inferences about realities existing outside experience. In order to provide this basis, cause-and-effect must be taken as a *natural* relation. But in consequence, everything applies to it that has been established about imagination, operating under the influence of association. The natural relation whereby we can make causal inferences beyond experience is due to a union, established by regulated imagination, among ideas that are unconnected in their own nature.

The findings of Sections 4 and 5, above, may be summarized in one phrase: *the loosening of ideas*. Ideas are loosened by showing the power of imagination over distinct, separable ideas and by reducing the philosophical relation of cause-and-effect to impotence. Detached ideas permit of no inference whatever, since they are perfectly uninformative concerning objects lying beyond sense experience. The only way to rehabilitate causal inference is to overcome the loosening of ideas. This can be done by recognizing the stabilizing effect of custom upon imagination and, consequently, by appealing to the natural associative powers operating in the mind itself to build up natural relations. The result is, however, that causal inference is a form of moral reasoning and can achieve only moral certitude or probability. All this is established by Hume even before he begins his formal examination of cause. He has succeeded in framing the question in such a way that his own answer is inevitable, within the given framework.

6. THE ANALYSIS OF CAUSE

In his discussion of the idea of cause and our belief in it, Hume drew generously upon the criticisms offered by the skeptics, Hobbes, Malebranche, and Berkeley. But although he often echoed his predecessors, even in the choice of words, he produced a unified and powerful critique of his own, which affected the principle of causality as such and did not stop short at some particular instance of causation. He began by asking whether the idea of cause is derived from some qualities in the objects themselves (the original sense impressions) or from some relation among the objects. The former alternative is excluded without much consideration. Whatever *intrinsic quality* one may choose as characterizing cause, one may also find an object that lacks this quality and yet figures in a causal connection. Hence the search turns toward the various *relations* among objects. Among the philosophical relations that bear upon matters of fact, there are three that seem to enter into the notion of cause-and-effect: *contiguity, temporal priority,* and *necessary connection.* The objects related as cause-and-effect are in some contact; the object designated as cause enjoys a temporal priority over the effect; there is a necessary link between the two terms. Hume did not give a serious hearing to causal theories in which contiguity and temporal priority do not belong to the essential conditions of the causal relation. But he did grant that, although these notes are components in the causal relation, they are not its sole and sufficient constituents. There are cases where objects are contiguous and related according to a temporal series, and yet where the relation of cause-and-effect is absent.

Hence the main investigation concerns the origin of the idea of a necessary connection. There are two ways of tracing it to its source. The first is a *logical* examination of its role in the general principle of causality; the second is a *psychological* description of how it arises in the mind, in the case of particular causal inferences. Hume's analysis will be given according to these two stages, logical and psychological, reserving criticism of his argument for a third division.

1. The previous *logical* defenses of causality made by Hobbes, Clarke, and Locke provide Hume with a set of easy targets. The common objection he makes is that his predecessors suppose the need for a cause, in the very proofs they advance to establish this need. He takes as a generally received statement of the causal principle Locke's dictum: *Whatever begins to exist, must have a cause of existence.*[17] Locke's justification of this proposition rests upon his analysis of the idea of power, which alone provides the transition from observed beginnings to the relation of cause-and-effect. From Hume's

---

[17] *Ibid.,* I, iii, 3 (Selby-Bigge, 78; cf. 79–82, 157, for Hume's criticism).

standpoint, there are two insuperable objections to Locke's argument. First, Locke jumps directly from experiences of beginnings to the rational inference that powers must be present. But this implies that the idea of power is *original to reason*. This contradicts the empirical principle that ideas derive not directly from reason but from some impression given in experience. Since Locke does not identify the original impression, Hume concludes that the idea of causal power either has no empirical origin or has a source in a direction where Locke fails to look. Hume himself accepts the second alternative, but postpones examination of it until the psychological study of particular instances of causal belief.

His second criticism of Locke is directly damaging against the accepted formulation of the causal principle. He contends that *"reason, as distinguished from experience,* can never make us conclude, that a cause or productive quality is absolutely requisite to every beginning of existence."[18] Italics have been added, in making this quotation, so that Hume's position will not be misunderstood. His purpose is to show, not that the relation of cause-and-effect is groundless, but rather that it cannot be validated by *abstract reason,* acting apart from experience. Since reason acts in this way only when it is making mathematical or ideal demonstrations, Hume has already ruled out the abstract use of reason as a method to be employed in determining causal matters of fact. Hence the point of his second objection is that no *demonstrative* proof can be made of the principle of causality. This follows because demonstration is limited to the relations among ideas, whereas no reasoning from mere ideas can establish the need of a real cause and the necessary, existential connection between cause and effect.

Demonstrative proof is such that a denial of the conclusion entails a contradiction. All of Hume's critical remarks on the causal principle are intended to show that it can be denied, without leading to a logical contradiction. In his main logical doctrine on separability and existence, he has already set the stage for proving this thesis. The *ideas* of cause and effect are distinct and separable from each other — otherwise we beg the issue and label them correlative notions. Hence it is entirely possible for imagination to divorce the idea of a cause from that of a beginning of existence. It is then "easy for us to conceive any object to be non-existent this moment, and existent the next,

---

[18] *A Treatise of Human Nature,* I, iii, 14 (Selby-Bigge, 157).

without conjoining to it the distinct idea of a cause."[19] Since a causeless beginning of existence is conceivable by imagination, without involving a contradiction, the opposite of the causal principle is possible, as far as the *objective, logical content of ideas* is concerned. This eliminates any strict demonstration of the principle, since a demonstration concludes to that, the opposite of which cannot be consistently conceived. We must look elsewhere than to demonstrative reasoning about ideas for the source of the idea of a necessary connection.

Rather indignantly, Hume once told one of his correspondents that he never maintained the absurd proposition that anything might arise without a cause, but only held that the certainty of the falsehood of such a causeless beginning cannot be obtained by intuition or demonstration.[20] From his own standpoint, his protest is justified in two ways. First, the word *things* is equivocal, since it may refer either to beings as they exist outside of our perceptions or to the immediate objects of our experience: the impressions and ideas. Hume's discussion is confined to "things" in the second sense, as objects-in-cognition, whereas his opponents were referring to the extramental existents. He does refer sometimes to the secret causes operating in nature, but such references have no strict empirical standing and can only lead to the Kantian problem of how we can affirm the reality of unknowable things. In the second place, Hume does not champion causeless beginnings, even among things or objects taken in his sense of the word. He is only concerned with showing the *nondemonstrative, extralogical* nature of our rejection of the idea of a causeless beginning. In regard to matters of fact, abstract reasoning about mere ideas is the same as the play of imagination in separating distinct ideas. The case for causality would be hopeless, were demonstrative certainty the only alternative to complete skepticism. But the moderate or true

---

[19] *Ibid.*, I, iii, 3 (Selby-Bigge, 79). In "Professor Stace and the Principle of Causality," *The New Scholasticism*, 24 (1950), 398–416, F. X. Meehan criticizes Hume and his contemporary exponent, W. T. Stace, for inferring from one's ability to *imagine* an object without *imagining* its cause, that therefore one can *conceive* of an object as *coming to be* without *any* cause.

[20] *Letter of February, 1754*, in *The Letters of David Hume* (edited by J. Y. Greig, I, 187). Hume deals with "things" or "facts," only in the sense of the contents of our statements about the occurrence or regularities of our perceptions. Since these statements can succeed each other without any ontological dependence among themselves, he finds no objective basis in his "facts" for the causal inference. The first task of realism is to distinguish unequivocally between the Humean fact and the act of being, on the part of the existent thing. See M. O'Donnell, "Hume's Approach to Causation," *Philosophical Studies*, 10 (1960), 64–99.

skeptic, finding the justification of his causal belief blocked off in the direction of demonstrative reason and the intrinsic nature of ideas, may still turn to the area of disciplined imagination, moral reasoning, and probable assurance. The constructive side of Hume's argument is manifested when he shifts to a psychological discussion of particular instances of causal inference. His purpose is not to deny their existence but to explain them on other than demonstrative grounds.

2. From the *psychological* standpoint, a cause may be defined as *"an object followed by another, and whose appearance always conveys the thought to that other."*[21] What is the source of the inference that leads the mind from this cause to this effect, say, from flame to heat? What is given in a particular encounter is a flame conjoined with heat: each is a distinct object or perception. But we notice that, after this experience is repeated several times, it is no longer necessary to furnish both objects. Upon the presentation of but one of them by sense or memory, the understanding will recall the other. It will do so in conformity with the past experience, and will relate the objects in necessary connection, as cause and effect. On the side of the objects themselves, there has been perceived only a contiguity and temporal succession. The source of the necessary connection must be sought on the side of the mental operations: in the *repetition* of the experience of contiguity and temporal sequence. We affirm a necessary connection between the two objects, joined in the natural relation of cause-and-effect, because we have experienced them in constant — or rather, in *frequent — conjunction*. The leap from factual conjunction to necessary-connection-in-virtue-of-a-causal-power is made by the mind, acting involuntarily under the force of habitual association. Imagination or the understanding makes a *customary union* between the ideas of flame and heat. Hence it can make a confident inference even in regard to what heat will do in the future, although the particular case has not yet been experienced.

The causal inference rests not upon a *connection perceived in the*

---

[21] *An Enquiry concerning Human Understanding*, VII, 2 (Selby-Bigge, 77). One of Hume's major psychological arguments against Locke is that we do not even experience real causation on the part of our own will. This assertion was challenged by the French philosopher, Maine de Biran, who declared that we must approach the facts of interior life with a specially proportioned attitude (the *sens intime*), and not measure them exclusively in terms of external events (through the *sens externe*). For Biran's criticism, see P. P. Hallie, "Maine de Biran and the Empiricist Tradition," *The Philosophical Quarterly*, I (1950–1951), 152–64.

objects but upon one *instituted by the mind,* operating in accordance with the principles of association. Repetition of given conjunctions "causes or produces" (at least, Hume allows that this one instance of active causation is given!) a definite set or mental determination. The mind acquires a feeling of being constrained to pass from the one idea to the other, and to link them necessarily through a causal power. This *determination of mind or feeling of a necessity* to make the causal inference constitutes the causal belief and is the source of the idea of a necessary connection. Although this idea does not arise from any impression of sensation, it does have an empirical origin in an *impression of reflection:* in the felt necessity to pass from the one idea to the other.[22] The only necessity lies in the mind so constrained, not in the objects. Thus an empirical but nonobjective explanation is given of the genesis of our idea of cause and the causal belief.

Repetition of the experience of conjunction does not *increase insight* into any relation among the objects but only *generates a habit* of mind to link them together. The connecting principle remains unintelligible, since it operates "naturally" only to produce the custom of associating the ideas, rather than to reveal dependencies in being. The only difference lies in the manner in which the conjoined ideas eventually come to strike the mind. Under the impetus of custom, the conjunction addresses itself more forcefully and vivaciously to the mind, thus approximating to the strength of an original impression of sense. The impression of reflection or feeling of constraint is (to use the language of Malebranche) a *je-ne-sais-quoi,* that makes the mind believe in the causal connection. Hence the causal inference becomes a *settled belief,* that may be integrated with the rest of the system of reality, developed by imagination and the force of association. It never attains the absolute certainty of scientific knowledge, but it is more than a reckless conjecture. It gives sufficient assurance to shape our practical life with sagacity. Yet Hume admits that his explanation cannot still the doubts of a skeptical mind, whose goal is strict knowledge or nothing at all. Whatever the strength of probability behind any causal belief, the fact remains that *"even after the observation of the frequent or constant conjunction of objects, we have no reason to draw any inference concerning any object beyond those of which we have had experience."*[23] Not an abstract reason

22 *A Treatise of Human Nature,* I, iii, 14 (Selby-Bigge, 155–156); *An Enquiry concerning Human Understanding,* VII, 2 (Selby-Bigge, 74–75).
23 *A Treatise of Human Nature,* I, iii, 12 (Selby-Bigge, 139). Malebranche's influence

but a customary inclination is the basis for making the causal inference. Belief in the presumed likeness between what we have experienced and have not experienced is a practical necessity; we cannot demonstrate it and yet we cannot live without accepting and acting upon it.

3. A critical appraisal of this theory may point out, first, that its greatest service is to have brought out into the open an *inherent conflict* between rational and empirical motives that had been troubling British philosophy for a century. Hume illustrated this conflict in the central instance of causality, upon which so many fundamental doctrines rest. His analysis could only be made within a philosophical tradition nourished by two major disjunctions: between reason and experience, and between ideal demonstration and existential belief. Hume's skepticism was a vigilant refusal to confuse the members of these disjunctions or to water down the basic oppositions. His skeptical attitude was a "mitigated" one, only insofar as he made provision for coherent experience and reliable action even within the context of these antitheses.

The opposition between *reason* and *experience* dominates Hume's treatment of cause-and-effect. Of the former power, he offers a caricature that even an enthusiastic Cartesian would find difficult to recognize. In its metaphysical employment, reason is supposed to operate in a purely abstract and a priori way, entirely apart from the guidance of sense observation. Its insights are attained effortlessly and penetrate at once into the very essences of things, laying bare, in a definitive and unalterable way, the entire causal order of the universe. Hume finds it easy to puncture these inflated claims, but he has no right to ask that a valid conception of empirical understanding be governed solely by opposition to *this view* of reason. Reason may be regarded in a moderate way, as working in closest dependence upon the deliverances of sense, as relying upon patient observation of the natural world, and as recognizing that its findings are never exhaustive of the nature of things. Between reason, so understood, and experience a breach need never occur, since reason is then a major component in shaping a humane sort of experience. In point of fact, Hume never succeeds in realizing his own ideal of "experimental reasoning," since he is unable to integrate reason with sense and imagination, without depriving reason of its distinctive function

upon Hume's causal theory has been assessed by R. W. Church, "Malebranche and Hume," *Revue Internationale de Philosophie*, 1 (1938–1939), 143–161.

within the whole and thus reducing it to the status of a captive, habit-dominated imagination.

In respect to the causal problem, the key assertion is that *"causes and effects are discoverable, not by reason but by experience."*[24] This statement contains an amphibology, since it can mean either that experience *rather than* reason discovers causal relations or that reason *apart from* experience *cannot* discover them. The latter meaning is perfectly compatible with the realistic view that reason must draw from an experimental source its original data about causation and the causal principle. Hume's intent, however, is to assign causal belief to a type of experience from which reason is barred. He has in mind the operations of what he likes to call "abstract reason, derived from inquiries *a priori*."[25] And it must be granted that this nonexperiential sort of reason does not discover causal relations. This was a commonplace with Malebranche and other Cartesians, who pointed out that, if material substance is a passive, extended thing, then no amount of rational analysis of this inert object can show real causation among created things. But to affirm that a supposedly autonomous a priori reason cannot discover causal relations, is still to leave unaffected the rational power, as it actually functions in human experience. For, the rational principle in experience co-operates with the sensory powers, so that it may discover — with their aid and yet in a distinctively intellectual way — causal relations furnished by the beings of our experience. Hume is systematically prevented from recognizing this aspect, since he restricts the valid function of reason to abstract, mathematical calculation. In causal inference, he can make room for the understanding only by reducing it to the imagination, as stabilized by associative bonds.

---

[24] *An Enquiry concerning Human Understanding,* IV, 1 (Selby-Bigge, 28). For a sustained Aristotelian-Thomistic criticism, read Marie-de-Lourdes, R. J.-M., "Essai de commentaire critique sur l'*Enquiry concerning Human Understanding* de David Hume," *Laval Théologique et Philosophique,* 2 (1946), 1–78.

[25] *Dialogues concerning Natural Religion,* IV (Smith, 160); compare J. Dewey's similar remarks about speculative reason, in *Logic: The Theory of Inquiry,* 87. Hume is correct in rejecting the rationalistic, Leibnizian employment of sufficient reason and causality as purely a priori and deductive principles. Relying solely upon the formal necessity of these principles, we can make no analytically certain deductions about finite existents. This does not lead, however, to Hume's postulatory phenomenalism, since the intellect can grasp being and the experientially warranted necessities imposed by actually existing finite beings. We can base the causal inference upon the exigencies of finite existents, thus avoiding both rationalism and phenomenalism. Consult E. Gilson, "Les principes et les causes," *Revue Thomiste,* 52 (1952), 39–63.

The second general contrast — between *ideal demonstration* and *existential belief* — springs from the first. It follows from the doctrine that the immediate object of experience is the mental percept and that a strict rational science is based on purely ideal connections. On Hume's part, there is no critical revision of this common patrimony of Descartes and Locke, but only an attempt to work out its radical implications. On this rationalistic basis, he legitimates reason only as a mathematical, *non*metaphysical function and, by the same token, disqualifies it from making any existential and causal inquiries. He is following a sound lead, when he distinguishes between mathematical and causal investigations, and when he regards the latter as existential or bearing on matter of fact. It is also true that many problems, concerning matters of fact and particular causal connections, cannot be settled with more than probable assurance. But it is something else to hold that the causal principle itself has *no* demonstrative foundation and that causal inferences *never* give more than probable assurance.

The Humean notion of *demonstration* would rule out every attempt to make a demonstrative causal inference. But the view that a demonstration is excluded, as long as the contrary of a matter of fact is conceivable, suffers from two defects: one, *historical,* and the other, *theoretical.* Newton (whose method Hume adopts) had faced the contention that, since the Cartesian vortexes are conceivable, they present a serious alternative explanation of the world and detract from the certainty of his own conclusions. His rule against using abstract hypotheses in natural philosophy was intended to undermine arguments based merely upon what is conceivable, according to scientific imagination. In regard to matters of fact, demonstrations are not disturbed merely by pointing out logically possible alternatives. Conclusions in natural philosophy are always open to further revision, not because of the abstract possibility of thinking given facts as nonexistent but only because research is always revealing further existential facts, bearing on the issue.

From the *theoretical* standpoint, it is difficult to determine whether Hume is referring to the contrary or the contradictory opposite. In either case, he argues as though the contingent matter of fact were the *conclusion* rather than the *point of departure* for causal reasoning, or as though it were a point of departure *only as a member of a temporal series*. It is true that any contingent existent can cease to be, but under the supposition of its actual existence it cannot be

regarded as nonexistent, here and now. What has to be explained is its
actual existence as a given fact: this is the beginning rather than the
end of the inference. Although the thing could either be or not be,
the given situation is that it actually does exist, in a contingent way.
It is this determinate matter of fact that requires explanation through
a present, actual, *per se* cause of its being. Viewed in this way, a
demonstration can be made from a contingent matter of fact to a
cause it must have, whatever we may imagine about its temporal
antecedents or consequents.

Hume is distracted from the proper question by his notion that
causal reasoning always concerns a *prediction* about future consequences or a *recapture* of temporal antecedents. He takes this tempo-
ralistic view of causal inference, since he has in mind the Lockean
arrangement of ideas and Newtonian scientific reasoning in which
the locating of an event in a temporal series is of prime importance.
Now, within this context, the ability of imagination to isolate an
event from its temporal connections would render the Lockean formulation of the causal principle meaningless. It would also block the
operation of the associative process, as described by Hume. But it
would leave intact the need for a cause to explain the actual existence
of whatever being is *presently given*. This latter exigency is independent of the question of prediction and retrospection. The only conclusion Hume might legitimately draw from the isolating power of
imagination is that it reveals the inadequacy of Locke's statement of
causality and also the discrepancy between Hume's scientific relation
of cause-and-effect and the actual causal inference about existent things.

Hume admits that the ability of imagination to conceive of distinct
objects as separately coming into existence, without invoking the
idea of a cause, does not bear upon real conditions. It is only the
obverse side of the inability of abstract reason to find intrinsic causal
connections among objects of perception. But the Humean matter of
fact or existence refers back no farther than to the original impressions
and their ideas. The only reason why imagination is free to conceive
of a causeless entrance into existence, is that the *new existent* is no
more than a *percept-object*. To save our sanity about belief in the
reality of such percept-objects, Hume turns to the natural, subjective
forces working coherently through imagination. But he does not come
to close grips with the problem presented by an existential judgment
about things, insofar as they exercise a *contingent act of being,* apart
from our perceptions. Hume has no distinctive existential judgment

and hence no *rational* ground in experience for cause-and-effect, as bearing upon the need for an influx of being in actual things.

Consequently, there are two sharply divergent ways of interpreting Hume's dictum that causal reasoning goes "beyond the evidence of our memory and senses."[26] On a realistic view, this would mean that sense and memory convey more data than they themselves are formally able to appreciate. Reason would then be said to grasp the significance of sensory deliverances for the question of the being of things, and thus to attain its own distinctive aspect of the object, through and in the empirical materials. Working along with sense, the human intellect would apprehend the given, contingent matter of fact, precisely in respect to its *dependence for being.* This would constitute a foundation for the causal inference — a foundation provided by the sensorily grasped fact and discerned by reason, from the distinctive standpoint of the participated existence or act of being that requires causal explanation. In Hume's reading of the situation, however, the understanding is simply *outrunning the objective evidence,* instead of seizing upon given connections and implications. Sense and memory tell us only about perceptual objects that can be rendered loose and unconnected, as far as their objective content is concerned. It is in spite of the atomistic reduction of sense evidence, that the Humean understanding can establish causal connections and make inferences from the natural relation of cause-and-effect. The conflict, in Hume's mind, between skeptical analysis and causal belief is brought into sharp relief in connection with the major types of causal inference in metaphysics.

7. EXTERNAL BODIES AND THE PERSONAL SELF

Hume regards metaphysics as an effort to prove the existence of three supraempirical objects: the world of external bodies, the personal self, and God. One purpose of his elaborate discussion of causality is to provide the principles of criticism for evaluating these three claims of metaphysics. He declares that his critique of metaphysics does not tell against the *reality* of external bodies, the personal self, and God, but only against philosophical assertions of having *knowl-*

---

[26] *An Enquiry concerning Human Understanding,* IV, 1 (Selby-Bigge, 26). For a realistic defense of the co-operation of sense and reason, in the apprehension of causation, cf. D. J. Hawkins, *Causality and Implication* (London, Sheed and Ward, 1937), Chap. IV: "Direct Apprehension of Implication and Causation" (65–88, with special reference to Hume and Kant).

edge about their existence. His argument is aimed at showing that our conviction about them is a matter of probability and natural belief, rather than of scientific demonstration. The tomes of metaphysics can safely be consigned to the flames, without loss, since they contain neither mathematical demonstrations about quantity and number nor an empirical analysis of the natural grounds of belief (v.g., imagination and association). Metaphysics can acquire no foothold in a system that reduces our knowledge of existence to an awareness of the percept as an object being perceived.

1. *Bodies in the External World.* Hume acknowledges that everyone begins by believing, blindly and instinctively, that material things exist apart from ourselves and would continue to exist, even if our percipient organism were removed. But this naïve conviction was challenged by Locke, who posited a *double* sort of existence: first, of the ideas as immediate objects of perception and, then, of the extramental things in the world. This theory of a double existence was challenged, in its turn, by Berkeley's criticism of primary qualities and material substance. Hume now seeks to eliminate Berkeley's own position, by furnishing a completely empirical account of belief in the external world, in which the intervention of God, as the supplier of stable ideas of sense, is rendered superfluous. He analyzes this belief into two related affirmations: that bodies enjoy a *continued* existence, and that they enjoy a *distinct* existence.[27] The problem is to discover whether belief in the continued and distinct existence of bodies is due to sense, reason, or imagination. In principle, the issue has already been decided, through Hume's attitude toward existence and existential inference.

By giving a special definition of *continued* existence, he has no difficulty in showing that it is never perceived by the *senses*. Continued existence cannot become the object of sense perception, since the kind of continuance meant here is a persistence that would remain, even after the senses cease to perceive it. Here, Hume is adopting the same type of argument that led Berkeley to the fallacy of the egocentric predicament. He defines continued existence (just as Berkeley defined extramental existence) as that which would persist, after every perception of it ceased — and then concludes that the

---

[27] *A Treatise of Human Nature,* I, iv, 2 (187–199). Cf. A. Leroy, "Statut de l'objet extérieur dans la philosophie de Hume," *Revue Internationale de Philosophie,* 6 (1952), 199–212, and W. S. Hamond, "Hume's Phenomenalism," *The Modern Schoolman,* 41 (1963–1964), 209–226.

senses could not have a perception of such a state. His argument justifies no conclusion about existential continuation in being or even about our judgment on such continuance, except on the assumption that sensation can inform us only about "internal and perishing" impressions. It is this same phenomenalistic premise which enables Hume also to maintain that the senses give no information about a *distinct* and independent existence. If the original impressions of sense are single and nonrepresentative (nonintentional forms), they do not point beyond themselves and do not give rise to the idea of a double existence. *Reason* is also barred from making the inference upon which such an idea would rest. If reason identifies the perception and the object, it is meaningless to speak about an inference from the one to the other. If it distinguishes between them, it can never move from the existence of the perception to that of an independent object. For, this would depend upon a causal relation. It has already been shown that this relation is confined to the conjunctions among several perceptions, so that reason would have no basis for extending it to a conjunction between perceptions and nonperceptual, external objects.

We are left with *imagination* as the only source of belief in independent bodies. Our conviction about a continued bodily existence is based on a natural, habit-generated inference of imagination. Imagination or concrete understanding passes insensibly from awareness of the coherence and constancy of certain impressions to an affirmation of the coherence and constancy — and, therefore, the *continued* existence — of their supposed bodily counterparts. Imagination suggests, irresistibly, that bodies enjoy a continued existence. Any interruptions can then be assigned solely to my perceptions, whereas the continuity and identity belong to independent objects. Continuance of existence on the part of bodies, regardless of my perception, implies their *distinctness* from me and thus their independent reality in an external universe.

Having dissected this belief in the external world, Hume reminds himself of his leading principles. Impressions remain "internal and perishing"; perceptions, however much alike, are distinct and separable; there is no perceivable connection between perceptions and an independent bodily existence; hence there is no ground for the causal inference to bodies, except the coherence and constancy of the perceptions themselves. The whole edifice of our conviction about an independent material world rests on the supposition and lively belief of imagination, aroused by the resemblances among perceptions and by nothing more. In a skeptical mood, Hume confesses that at present:

> [I] am more inclined to repose no faith at all in my senses, or rather imagination, than to place in it such an implicit confidence. I cannot conceive how such trivial qualities of the fancy, conducted by such false suppositions, can ever lead to any solid and rational system. . . . Carelessness and in-attention alone can afford us any remedy. For this reason I rely entirely upon them; and take it for granted, whatever may be the reader's opinion at this present moment, that an hour hence he will be persuaded there is both an external and internal world.[28]

The wry humor of the last remark illustrates Hume's attitude of mitigated skepticism, which admits that nature provides relief against its most unpalatable findings. But the text also reveals the vast disproportion between Hume's epistemological principles and the convictions which they are supposed to illuminate and explain. These principles go as far as one can go, on the assumption that the mind's direct and primitive objects are "single," autonomous impressions, rather than sensible existents themselves. Hume himself detects the implausibility of the resultant attempt to explain ordinary views about the material world. For, it depicts that everyday realistic outlook as being based entirely on a shaky supposition about perceptions, rather than on the implications of the original existential judgment about the sensible thing, grasped precisely as another act of existing.

2. *The Personal Self.* Hume agrees with his British predecessors that a theory of self must be constructed in conformity with one's theory of mind, but he takes a more radically phenomenalistic view of mind than they do. *Mind* may be defined as "nothing but a heap or collection of different perceptions, united together by certain relations, and supposed, though falsely, to be endowed with a perfect simplicity and identity. . . . [It is] that connected mass of perceptions, which

---

28 *A Treatise of Human Nature,* I, iv, 2 (Selby-Bigge, 217–218). In this passage, Hume sounds a pragmatic note, testing even his own theories by their consequences for life. Hume began with the traditional empiricist view that the worth of ideas is determined by their *origin* in experience; but he came to see that, although all beliefs have some sort of empirical origin, they do not all have the same *consequences* for experience. This shift from what William James called retrospective empiricism to a prospective, pragmatic, or radical empiricism was never completed by Hume, who remained skeptical in the face of the breakdown of the familiar empiricist principle, in crucial cases. On the two empiricist strains in Hume's thought, see J. H. Randall, Jr., "David Hume: Radical Empiricist and Pragmatist," *Freedom and Experience* (edited by S. Hook and M. R. Convitz), 289–312.

constitute a thinking being."[29] The *substantiality* of the mind is conspicuous by its absence from this definition. If by substance is meant something which may exist by itself, then (at least, as far as the free play of imagination is concerned) every distinct perception, being capable of separation and separate existence, is a genuine substance. But if substance is said to be something entirely different from a perception, then we can have no idea of its nature and cannot raise questions about the immateriality and substantiality of the soul. Contrary to Locke's and Berkeley's contention, Hume states that perceptions are grasped *as distinct objects,* and hence never convey to the mind any evidence about their manner of inherence in a subject or even about their need for such inherence. Hence causal inference is not justified in arguing from a requirement that is lacking in empirical meaning. In this clash of opinion among the empiricists, Hume is relying once more upon a strictly phenomenalistic approach to perceptions and upon his logical doctrine about distinct perceptions. Perceptions are distinct not only from each other but also from any subject and, indeed, from any reference to a subject of inherence. This *reification of perceptions* is the extreme consequence of the analytic method and the notion of a percept-object.

From the same standpoint, we are barred from attributing *simplicity* and *identity* to the mind. The idea of identity would have to rest upon some impression that remains invariant throughout a lifetime; the idea of simplicity would suppose that some impression reveals an indivisible center of union for the moments of experience. Neither of these conditions can be satisfied in terms of the Humean theory of knowledge. When I enter intimately into what I call *myself,* Hume says, I always stumble upon some particular perception. I never catch myself without some perception, and neither do I come upon myself as anything but a bundle or collection of different perceptions, each succeeding the other with inconceivable rapidity. In face of this situation, only one set of conclusions is possible for the Humean logic, based on the loosening of ideas. Since each perception is a distinct existent, no substance is needed; since the perceptions are all different and successive, there is no identity or invariant sameness of being; since the perceptions comprising the self are many, the self is not a simple thing.

---

[29] *A Treatise of Human Nature*, I, iv, 2 (Selby-Bigge, 207). See T. Penelhum, "Hume on Personal Identity," *The Philosophical Review*, 64 (1955), 571–589.

As usual, Hume employs this failure on the part of abstract reason as a recommendation that we seek a binding principle on the side of the "natural" forces, operating through imagination. Thought is under some kind of constraint to pass from one given perception to the next, and thus to generate the self through this continuous transition. The *personal self* arises when, in reflecting upon a past series of perceptions, we feel that one perception naturally introduces the next. Personal identity is a powerful fiction, aroused by the circumstance that imagination is able to pass smoothly from one perceptual object to the next, and hence comes to regard the series as invariable and uninterrupted. The similarity in the mind's *act of apprehending* the different perceptions instigates imagination to affirm a continuous identity of the self, on the side of the *objects perceived*. The easy transition is made under the associative force of resemblance and the natural relation of cause-and-effect. Thus the self is "a system of different perceptions or different existences, which are linked together by the relation of cause and effect, and mutually produce, destroy, influence, and modify each other."[30] *Memory* is the source of personal identity, insofar as it summons up images resembling past perceptions and grasps the causal succession of our perceptions, in the direction of the past. *Passion* and concern extend the same frame of causal reference forward as well as backward, strengthening the easy passage of thought and the reflective feeling that the perceptions belong to an identical, personal self.

For once, however, this counterprocess of binding together what empirical analysis has loosened, fails to achieve the kind of unity to which our experience bears testimony. Hume observes that he cannot find a satisfactory explanation of the feeling of *belongingness*, on the basis of which imagination declares that all our perceptions belong to the same personal self.

> In short there are two principles, which I cannot render consistent; nor is it in my power to renounce either of them, viz., *that all our distinct perceptions are distinct existences,* and *that the mind never perceives any real connexion among distinct existences.* Did our perceptions either inhere in something simple and individual, or did the mind perceive some real connexion among them, there would be no difficulty in the case. For my part, I must plead the privilege of a skeptic, and confess, that this difficulty is too hard for my understanding.[31]

---

[30] *A Treatise of Human Nature,* I, iv, 6 (Selby-Bigge, 261).
[31] *Ibid.,* Appendix (Selby-Bigge, 636).

This is a disarmingly frank passage. Hume concedes that an adequate synthesis of empirical findings about the personal self requires a knowledge of substance and objective causal connections, in respect to man. But his own first principle about distinct perceptions, leading as it does to a divorce of abstract reason from experience, prevents him from admitting the reality of *substance* in man. His second principle about real connections leads to his skeptical theory of relations and rules out any objectively given *causal principle,* operative in mental life. Nevertheless, he cannot avoid using substantial and causal terms, when he describes the self as a bundle and as a self-perpetuating series of perceptions. Although he warns against the imagery, he finds it convenient to compare the mind both to a *theater,* upon whose (substantial) stage various appearances are presented, and to a *republic* that perpetuates itself (causally) through the successive generations of its members.

The perceptions belonging to "our" mind are not an indiscriminate heap but constitute an ordered system. On the side of the cognitive acts themselves, these perceptions are already ordered by reference to "ourselves" and "our" imagination, even before Hume can apply his theory of how imagination produces the personal unity of the self. In order to give a plausible account of the association of perceptual objects, he covertly *presupposes some personal center of reference or intimate belongingness* for the perceiving operations. His empirical explanation of the self implies the effective presence of certain substantial and causal factors, but his theory of knowledge prevents him from ever reconciling their reality with his own first principles.

Hume's passing remarks on immortality and freedom are consistent with his general view of knowledge and causality. No demonstration of *immortality* is possible, both because there is no clear idea of an immaterial, simple substance and because such demonstration would suppose that the causal principle can extend to a state that is, by definition, beyond present human experience. Hume admits that reason places man above the brutes but not that it guarantees his survival beyond this life. It is likely that man, like other animals, will lose consciousness and succumb to the universal frailty and dissolution of things. Neither immortality nor freedom has a bearing upon moral conduct, even if they could be established.

The only acceptable meaning of *freedom* is that of a power of acting or not acting, according to the determination of the will.[32]

[32] See *An Enquiry concerning Human Understanding,* Section VIII: "Of Liberty and

Hume defines the will — somewhat inconsistently, in view of his causal doctrine — as a cause or power giving rise to action. Hence it must conform with the general definition of a cause: it must have a *necessary* connection with its effect, the voluntary action. Since in his own system, the only ascertainable necessary connection is one established by imagination or habituated understanding, Hume stresses the necessity involved in *our knowledge* of human actions. Human history and practical wisdom reveal large uniformities in human conduct, based on a constant conjunction between certain motives and certain voluntary actions. Hence we customarily draw an inference from motives and circumstances to character and action. As for the subjective sense of freedom, Hume traces it to a feeling of looseness among ideas which sometimes steals over us, either when we reflect upon the past or when we are performing actions. The agent who feels his actions to be subject only to his will, and his will to be subject to no necessity, is simply overlooking his own motives, especially that of displaying freedom.

The curious turn of Hume's speculations on freedom indicates the straits in which he is placed, whenever he attempts to apply his general principles to any particular areas of our experience. He argues from a determination in the *spectator's knowledge* to a determinism of the *agent's conduct*. There are several reasons, however, why this inference cannot rule out freedom of choice. In the first place, Hume's causal doctrine maintains that the necessity of the connection involved in a causal inference has a *subjective* source, in the habits of mind generated in the observer through repetition of frequent conjunctions. Such repetition does not render any more intelligible or any more determined the nature of the objective relation between the things conjoined in a causal judgment. Hence a constantly observed conjunction between human motives and actions can generate a necessity on the observer's part, but this determination provides no ground for attributing any necessary connection between the action and the motives or circumstances affecting the agent himself. Second, the causal inference concerns matter of fact. Consequently, on Hume's own principles, the only type of necessity that is involved in historical and statistical inferences is a moral one. If such a moral necessity could be transferred from the associative habits of

---

Necessity" (Selby-Bigge, 80–103). That the foreseeability of some free acts does not destroy their freedom, is shown by Y. Simon, "On the Foreseeability of Free Acts," *The New Scholasticism*, 22 (1948), 357–370.

the spectator to the elections of the agent, it would not eliminate the free nature of the choice. Moral necessity has no more than a probable weight, and this *probability* is compatible with human freedom. Third, free choice is not eliminated by noting that human actions always have motives and that men often act in similar ways, in view of similar motives and circumstances. This observation is incompatible only with a position that identifies freedom with passive indifference and motiveless action. The point at issue is not the *presence* and influence of motives, but the precise *way* in which motives do influence the elective act. Finally, the remark that one's conviction of being free is explainable by the desire for a conspicuous display of freedom, raises the question of how the desire to display a nonexistent freedom can mysteriously arise in human experience. The personal conviction about freedom is not due to a vague feeling of looseness among ideas or a self-deceiving desire. It arises through reflection upon the actual exercise of reason's positive domination over its practical judgment, concerning motives and circumstances of action.

8. GOD AND RELIGION

Hume's *Dialogues concerning Natural Religion* deals mostly with the current proofs for God's existence. Clarke's statement of the proofs (*Discourse concerning the Being and Attributes of God,* 1705) is taken as the standard argument, and no attempt is made to examine more rigorous demonstrations. Clarke furnishes an a priori and an a posteriori proof. The so-called a priori one is a conflation of a number of current arguments. It states that every effect must have a cause, that we must come eventually to an uncaused cause of the whole series, and that this first cause must necessarily exist (since it contains within itself its own reason of being). The a posteriori argument is one from design (not the older teleological argument), in which the order, beauty, and harmony of the universe are cited as proof of the existence of an intelligent and benevolent Author of nature. As for their probative force, Clarke maintains that the first argument is as cogent and certain as the simplest mathematical proposition, and that the second is so obvious that no man can be excused from giving assent to it.

As usual, Hume concentrates upon the claim to *knowledge* of God's existence. He shows very easily the inaptness of the comparison between mathematical reasoning and the a priori proof, because of the *nonexistential* character of the mathematical type of inference.[33] Furthermore, he challenges the possibility of making any demonstration concerning such a matter of fact as God's existence. He declares that, for man, the words "necessary existence" are without consistent meaning and cannot signify the outcome of any demonstrative process. Nor can any a priori argument settle an existential question, which involves a bond among ideas that cannot be derived from mere analysis of their objective content. In short, the entire Humean doctrine on reasoning and causality prevents him from accepting Clarke's first argument.

The a posteriori *argument from design* elicits from him, however, a much more elaborate analysis. Since there can be no existential demonstration, probability is all that can be expected from this proof. It is a *proof from analogy,* using the general principle: like effects, like causes. The degree of probability depends upon the closeness of similarity between the effects. In this instance, the constitution of nature is regarded as being analogous to a work of human art, with the inference that there exists a divine maker somehow similar to the human artisan.

Hume follows several lines of attack upon this contention, perhaps the most serious of which is that even *analogical reasoning* is out of place.[34] For it employs the relation of cause-and-effect which, to serve as a basis of inference, must be established through repeated observation of the conjunction between the objects. Every causal inference deals with *species* of objects, where the objects may be observed several times in conjunction. But in the argument from design, the world as a whole is a *unique* effect, which we do not observe to be repeated elsewhere. Furthermore we have no experience of the origin of worlds, similar to our repeated experience of the origin of works of art. The universe is an unparalleled effect and, being without parallel, does not permit an inference based on the analogy between similar effects. Hume adds that the order observed in the world may well be due to some immanent principle of life or world

---

[33] *Dialogues concerning Natural Religion,* IX (Smith, 188–192).

[34] *Ibid.,* II (Smith, 149–150); on the probable character of "analogical reasoning," cf. *A Treatise of Human Nature,* I, iii, 12 (Selby-Bigge, 142). In the *Dialogues,* Hume had in mind not only Clarke but also Anglican Bishop Joseph Butler, author of the popular *Analogy of Religion* (1736). Hume reduced the import of analogical reasoning almost to the vanishing point, where it became indistinguishable from his own philosophical skepticism. On the design argument among the Newtonians, see R. H. Hurlbutt, "David Hume and Scientific Theism," *Journal of the History of Ideas,* 17 (1956), 486–407.

soul, rather than to a cosmic mechanic. Perhaps nature should be conceived as an animated whole, a great organism, rather than as a huge machine of the Newtonian type.

Nevertheless, Hume admits that, upon observation of nature as a whole, and especially of parts like the eye, we are carried along by the feeling that there is some vague likeness between the cause of the universe and human intelligence. Hume sides neither with dogmatic atheists, in their outright *denial* of God's existence, nor with Deistic and orthodox rationalists, in their claim to have strictly *rational demonstrations*. It is "nature" or *inward feeling* upon which we rely, when the idea of an intelligent, divine contriver strikes us with the strength of a sensation. On the basis of the operation of unknown, customary, practical forces in human nature, Hume admits that he is inclined to accept this proposition: *"The cause or causes of order in the universe probably bear some remote analogy to human intelligence."*[35] But he hedges in his acceptance with a number of provisos. First, this proposition is incapable of demonstration and attains only a degree of *probability,* under pressure of the feeling of its fitness. Next, although we can affirm the existence of the intelligent cause of the world, we can never penetrate to its essential nature. Its inner being will always remain mysterious and closed off from inspection, so that the analogy from experience cannot be rendered less remote and indefinite. Analogical inference never leads to knowledge of the moral qualities of the universal, ordering mind: only the *natural* attribute of intelligence is established. God's *moral* attributes of justice, benevolence, mercy, and rectitude may be compatible with the being of an infinite mind, but the world of our experience provides no ground for affirming them. The disorder and evil in the universe do not encourage the feeling that the cosmic mind is a moral agent.

This leads to the third and most important qualification attached to the above proposition, viz., that it can sustain no inference bearing

[35] *Dialogues concerning Natural Religion,* XII (Smith, 227). Because of its dialogue form, this book does not reveal Hume's position in unequivocal fashion. The principle of interpretation used here is that, whereas the orthodox Demea of the *Dialogues* in no way reflects Hume's own mind, the author's attitude is expressed mainly by the moderate skeptic, Philo, and by Cleanthes, in the degree that the latter champions the promptings of nature. For other interpretations, see N. K. Smith's Introduction to his edition of the *Dialogues,* E. C. Mossner's "The Enigma of Hume," *Mind,* N.S., 45 (1936), 334–349, and B. M. Laing's "Hume's *Dialogues concerning Natural Religion,*" *Philosophy,* 12 (1937), 175–190. Also, R. J. Butler, "Natural Belief and the Enigma of Hume," *Archiv für Geschichte der Philosophie,* 42 (1960), 73–100.

on human life and specific plans of action or forbearance. Only a "plain, philosophical assent," *purely theoretical in import,* can be given to the statement about God's existence. This is of the greatest moment for Hume, since it enables him at one stroke to define true religion, criticize existing religions, and keep religion entirely apart from morality. Belief in the existence of a supreme, intelligent mind may be called the religious hypothesis, but no new fact can ever be inferred from this hypothesis and no practical decision affected by it. In this sense, Hume speaks of *true religion* as being a species of philosophy: it is a cognitive assent to God's existence (under the above conditions), and nothing more. Philosophical religion admits no revelation, no rites, no miracles, no special merit or demerit, no distinctively religious duties or feelings. It consists entirely and exclusively in the empirical, speculative assent to theism, without entailing any repercussions upon human conduct and ethical judgment.

Obviously, this rarefied attitude will always be confined to the few and is a far cry from what is usually called religion. In his *Natural History of Religion,* Hume attempted to trace back the popular conception of religion to its sources in human nature, as he has described it. *Religion* is not universal and uniform enough to be a primary instinct of man, but it is founded upon such primary passions as his fear of natural disaster and his hope for betterment. These passions are not themselves specifically religious, but become so when they are directed toward a certain object: an *invisible, intelligent power.* Religious feelings develop from the responses of hope-and-fear to belief in this object. Hume thought that religions were originally polytheistic and that they only gradually hit upon the notion of one, infinite power. Religious monotheism happens to coincide with the best philosophical view of God. But Hume's early training was such that he could never think about actual religions in an objective and balanced spirit. He constantly warned against their "superstition and fanaticism," refusing to tolerate any alliance between organized religion and philosophy.

Hume's theory of God and religion has a sharply limited theoretical range and yet has exercised great historical influence. As a criticism of the theistic arguments popular in Newtonian circles, it exposes their lack of logical rigor and their failure to secure any metaphysical foundations. Clarke offers no adequate defense of causality and no theory of existential demonstration. He fails to present a thoroughgoing a posteriori demonstration, based upon causation, contingency, and finality. Hume, in turn, gives such arguments no attention, on the ground that they are ruled out, in principle, by his previous treatment of demonstration, existence, and causality. Any fundamental criticism of his position must make a similar return to these underlying epistemological and metaphysical issues, especially to the nature of existential demonstration and the application of the causal principle to beings in their own reality (and not merely to our percepts). Furthermore, the distinction must be underlined between the Thomistic metaphysical doctrine on the analogical predication of being and the meaning of analogy found in Butler, Clarke, and Hume. The latter thinkers regard analogical reasoning as a manner of making loose comparisons, based on a fairly wide sampling of instances. As so defined, it could never be employed in strict demonstration but must be reserved for probable reasoning. Hume's suggestion that even analogical reasoning to God's existence is illegitimate, because of its application of the relation of cause-and-effect to the unique act of creation, is illuminating. For it is a reminder that Hume's "natural relation" of cause-and-effect rests upon the mechanism of repetition and habit, rather than upon intellectual apprehension of the essential dependence-for-being of one existent thing upon another. Clearly, the major problem lies in Hume's general conception of cause rather than in his particular application of it to inference about God's existence.

Hume's notion of religion marks a turning point from Deism to some of the later naturalistic tendencies in the philosophy of religion. He completed the process of reducing religion to its natural, philosophical content. At the same time, he disagreed with the Deists about the exact nature of that content. Belief in God rests on feeling, imagination, and custom, rather than on abstract reason. To this extent, Hume prepared the way for the nineteenth-century stress upon the *emotional bases* of the religious attitude. But he refused to allow any practical influence to be exerted by the religious hypothesis. It is a belief generated by feeling and yet restricted to the speculative order, like so many other convictions that have a similar origin in the natural forces of the mind. By refusing to permit belief in an infinite mind to serve as a legitimate, animating principle of human conduct, Hume gave new impetus to two historical trends. He contributed toward the gradual *severance* of religious motives from the central concerns of a secular, Western civilization, and he prepared for a *naturalistic morality* entirely divorced from religious considerations. Although he realized that this quarantine of religion can never be made complete, Hume did his best to reduce the area of religion's effectiveness, by suggesting that the affairs of life can be organized without reference to God, whose existence is likely but whose moral nature remains completely enigmatic to men. Conversely, any effective restoration of theistic and religious influences in our present world depends, in some measure, upon showing that human knowledge is not confined within the limits set by Hume's empiricist premises.

9. PASSIONS AND MORAL PRINCIPLES

Although later philosophers have given the lion's share of their attention to Hume's theory of the understanding, he himself regarded his theory of the passions and morals as the goal and completion of his philosophy of human nature. In a way, his moral doctrine is the answer to a dare, formulated in the speculative portions of his thought: Granted that we cannot base our actions upon an afterlife, freedom, or God — nevertheless show that human life can be conducted wisely and well. Hume accepts this challenge by rounding out his chain of reasoning and system of the sciences with a theory of passions and morals.

Hume is confident that the Newtonian method of experimental reasoning can be extended into the region of the *passions*.[36] He supposes them to be governed by a regular mechanism, which permits one to explain them by means of a few, general principles. The passions are taken to be natural states, in the sense of being fairly constant and uniform, not only within one individual's experience but also among all men. The distinction between primary impressions of sensation and secondary impressions of reflection may now be put to a new use. For among the *primary impressions* are included not only sensory data but also bodily *pleasures* and *pains,* due directly to the operation of physical causes in the world. And the *secondary impressions* (derived either from primary ones or from their ideas) consist not only in the dispositions bearing on causal inference but also in the *passions*. Although derivative in nature, the passions are also original impressions, insofar as they are complete and nonrepresentative states. They may be divided into the *direct* and the *indirect passions,* depending upon whether they arise from

---

[36] Through application of the few, simple laws of association to the passions, Hume hoped to effect a Copernican revolution in moral philosophy; cf. *A Treatise of Human Nature*, II, i, 3–4 (Selby-Bigge, 282–284).

feelings of pleasure and pain or require the aid of some other qualities.

In treating of the *direct passions,* Hume speaks very briefly of some few that "arise from a natural impulse or instinct, which is perfectly unaccountable."[37] Our desire for an enemy's punishment or a friend's happiness is a primitive passion that precedes any particular experience of pleasure or pain, and that is, indeed, productive of such feelings. We have to exercise basic impulses of this sort in order to discover, through experience, what things satisfy or thwart them. For the most part, however, the direct passions do follow, naturally and with comparatively little preparation, from the pleasure and pain (i.e., good and evil), which we undergo or consider. Desire and aversion, grief and joy, hope and fear, are passions of this sort, moving a man by a direct and original instinct. Despite their importance as components of our passional life, Hume does not analyze them in much detail. His general principles of association and sympathy are better displayed in the growth of the indirect passions, upon which he bestows his main attention.

To treat of the *indirect passions* and their attendant qualities, Hume makes use of his phenomenalistic notions of self and cause. For, he finds that passions always have an object and a cause. There is an unmistakable difference between the *cause* or idea that arouses a passion, and the *object* toward which the passion, so excited, is directed. From the standpoint of their object, the indirect passions are divided into *self-regarding* and *other-regarding* ones. The object of the indirect passions of pride and humility is the self, i.e., "that succession of related ideas and impressions, of which we have an intimate memory and consciousness."[38] In the case of the indirect passions of love and hatred, the object is some person other than the self. The direction of these various passions to their respective objects is not only a *natural* (steady and universal) property but also an *original* one, a primary ordination that Hume does not care to resolve into anything more simple. Although all the causes of the passions are natural, they are not all original. We can think of a thousand causes — many of them produced by human art or good fortune — that lead us to feel pride and the other passions. But all the causes of passions share in common two general traits: the production of pleasure or pain, and a reference to ourselves or others. Now it happens that the passions themselves have two corresponding properties: their very

[37] *Ibid.,* II, iii, 9 (Selby-Bigge, 439).
[38] *Ibid.,* II, i, 2 (Selby-Bigge, 277).

essence is to be *a pleasant or painful sensation* and their orientation is *toward oneself or others.*

Hume does not attempt further analysis of this happy correspondence between the properties of the causes of passions and the properties of passions themselves. He accepts it as a descriptively ultimate fact, so that he may apply to it his *principles of association* and thus construct a *system* of the passions. There is a correlation between a double set of ideas and impressions, permitting an easy transition and blending to be made, on the basis of the resemblances within the two sequences. The cause of the passion is directed to the very same idea or object to which the passion itself is naturally ordained: the self or some other person. Similarly, the impression or sensation produced independently by the cause of the passion is a pleasure or pain, which therefore resembles the passion itself. Through a mutual reinforcement of the two associative bonds among ideas and passions, the mind is given a *double impulse.* This accounts for the passional strength of anything that both conveys pleasure or pain and also bears a reference to oneself or another. There is an easy transition from one idea to the next (the ideas acquiring vivacity from association with the impressions), and from one passion to the next. Once a passion is aroused, it is likely to call forth a whole train of similar ones, especially under the influence of the mind's consideration of various aspects and relations of the causes and objects involved.

Another major factor, along with the association of resembling ideas and passions, is the operation of *sympathy,* taken not only in the restricted sense of benevolence but also as a general ability to appreciate the similar feelings transpiring within other selves.[39] The individual is not constitutionally egoistic — on this point, Hume agrees with the criticism of Hobbes made by Hutcheson and the Moral Sense School. The individual has an ardent desire for society and a capacity to imagine how others are feeling. There is a sort of psychic contagion, by which a sentiment may run from one man to another. From the appearances of another, I can gain an idea of what he seems to be feeling. By bringing this idea into relation with my own self, it acquires the liveliness of an impression. Thus it arouses similar passions within myself, although always sympathetically, with regard to the other person and his passional state. Although admitting that

---

[39] *A Treatise of Human Nature,* II, i, 11; III, iii, 1 (Selby-Bigge, 316–324, 575–578); *An Enquiry concerning the Principles of Morals,* II (Selby-Bigge, 176–182).

his system of basic self-regarding and other-regarding passions requires many qualifications, Hume believed that its principles can account for the most subtle complexities of our emotional attitudes.

One consequence of this theory is that the rationalistic view of the pre-eminence of *reason over passion* must be abandoned. Like Hutcheson, Hume has in view an abstract sort of reason, modeled along mathematical lines and reliant solely upon general definitions and eternal verities, in dealing with practical problems. Clearly, such a reason is proximately unfitted for making practical decisions. By itself, this purely speculative reason can never provide a sufficiently powerful motive for will and cannot oppose passion. Hume admits that reason (taken in a more concrete and practical way) can exert an oblique or mediate influence upon the passions. But it does so only by directing the passions toward other causal relations and objects or by opening up new possibilities, rather than by producing original, practical impulses of its own. Only a contrary impulse can oppose a passion: hence it is meaningless to speak of the conflict between reason and passion. Even at its most effective, *"reason is, and ought only to be, the slave of the passions,* and can never pretend to any other office than to serve and obey them."[40] It may be an enlightened and privileged servitor, working along with the passions in an advisory and guiding capacity. But of itself, reason cannot be an original passional power, such that to think of a proper course of action is to execute it in fact.

Despite his extreme language, Hume is moving here toward a moderate position that recognizes the guiding function of practical reason, the distinctive contribution of the appetitive powers, and the need for the mutual impenetration of reason and the appetitive powers in human conduct. But he is hindered from achieving a balance among these factors, because of his denial of free choice, his preoccupation with the rationalistic view of reason, and his own difficulties about the relation between reason and experience. Hence he tends to give a watered-down conception of reason in its moral function, coalescing it with the relatively mild and moderate passions. The practical reduction of reason to the mild passions corresponds to the speculative reduction of reason to imagination. In neither case does Hume preserve the distinctive role of reason in human experience.

---

[40] *A Treatise of Human Nature,* II, iii, 3 (Selby-Bigge, 415; italics added).

Hume repudiated the view of Locke, Clarke, and Wollaston that ethical and mathematical reasoning are basically the same. Ethics has an *existential* bearing and, therefore, is nonmathematical and nondemonstrative. Like Hutcheson again, Hume emphasized the *empirical* and *probable* character of moral science (as the study of practical matters of fact), as well as the need to base moral judgments on another basis than abstract reason. Moral distinctions are not grounded primarily upon an eternal fitness of things but upon a *moral sense,* with which reason must co-operate.[41] In pronouncing an action virtuous or vicious, we rely upon the constitution of our own nature, which supplies the sentiment of approval or disapproval, satisfaction or uneasiness. Fortunately, this moral sense has been uniformly distributed among men, so that *universal* valuation, and not mere individual preference, is expressed in its judgments. Moreover, although the moral approval or disapproval is a matter of pleasure or pain, it is also a sentiment that considers the action or character of others for their own sake and apart from our individual interest. Thus a certain *impartiality* is achieved, along with the universality. By making these suppositions about the moral sense, Hume sought to avoid the moral subjectivism toward which the theory leads.

We give our moral approval either to what is immediately agreeable to ourselves or others, or else to what is useful to ourselves or others. Actions or characters that give us *pleasure* by their mere sight may be termed *virtuous* or morally good. But since moral approbation is based on agreement of an action with human sentiment, *utility* can also be used as a criterion of virtue.[42] In judging what is useful, reason is helpful, since it provides information about the various means at hand and takes account of the long-range bent of our passions. Sympathy, for instance, works hand-in-hand with self-interest. We have a native sense of humanity or fellow-feeling, which sympathy cultivates to the point of approving not only what is personally useful but also what is of public utility. The whole *system of justice,* contracts, property, and the state, arises artificially from human self-interest. But when we see that these arrangements affect the happiness of humanity at large, we are moved to an immediate, sym-

---

[41] *Ibid.*, III, i, 2 (Selby-Bigge, 470–476); *An Enquiry concerning the Principles of Morals,* I, and Appendix I (Selby-Bigge, 170–175, 285–294).

[42] *A Treatise of Human Nature,* III, iii, 1 (Selby-Bigge, 578–591); *An Enquiry concerning the Principles of Morals,* V (Selby-Bigge, 212–232).

pathetic response of pleasure or misery, approbation or disapprobation. In this way, social arrangements are estimated as being virtuous or vicious. Despite the *conventional* origin of our several obligations in justice, they are a continuation of natural tendencies and win approval at once, within a settled society.[43] Guided by reason, sympathy educates and strengthens the other-regarding impulses, so that the moral sense may include general approval of the interests of others on a social scale. The actions of men in society come to have moral significance through this immediate response of pleasure or displeasure, aroused by a contemplation of them.

Hume's ethics was transitional between the moral sense theories and the full-blown utilitarianism of Bentham and Mill. His adaptation of Hutcheson's view of moral sense enabled him to break with an ethics of abstract rules and eternal definitions, and to look for moral qualities in what affects our passions and impulses. But he did not think that there is a special sense, having as its object a special "moral" quality of things. Rather, he located moral distinctions in the impact of actions and characters upon our basic concerns, as expressed in a sentiment of agreeableness or disagreeableness. Utilitarianism looms on the horizon as an explanation of the good in terms of maximum happiness for the individual and society. But for Hume, utility and happiness are not sufficient measures of the moral good, unless they are integrated with a certain *contemplation* and *approval* of the springs of action leading to happiness, private and social. Kant's dissatisfaction with the Humean solution of the moral problem arose precisely at this juncture. For he was unable to see how approval of the agreeable can serve as a properly moral criterion, especially in situations where there is a conflict between agreeableness and obligation. Kant acknowledged that the feeling of approbation is a companion of moral judgment and action. But he pointed out that this accompanying circumstance does not establish the objectively valid principles upon which moral distinctions are based and in the light of which a man can choose a model or moral exemplar. The opposition between the Kantian ethic of duty and the utilitarian ethic of maximal happiness stems from their diverse estimations of Hume's account of moral judgments.

---

[43] Read B. Wand, "Hume's Account of Obligation," *Philosophical Quarterly*, 6 (1956), 155–168.

SUMMARY

Hume wanted to take the castle of human nature by storm, with the aid of the Newtonian method. He agreed with his empiricist predecessors that the immediate objects of the mind are its own contents or perceptions. But he added the qualification, taken from Newton, that scientific method cannot presume to give any knowledge about spiritual or material substances or any extramental order of essential causes. For a radical phenomenalism, our perceptions and their subjective connections are all that we can hope to know. Yet just as Newton was able to formulate uniform laws for all physical appearances, so Hume proposed the mechanical laws of association as regulative of all mental appearances. He distinguished between philosophical and natural relations, since some comparisons among ideas involve no connecting principle, whereas others rest upon a connecting bond. The philosophical relation of cause-and-effect has no independent status; its constitutive ideas are perfectly loose and provide no basis for metaphysical inferences beyond experience. Causal inferences are based upon the natural relation of cause-and-effect, in which the connecting bond must be traced back to custom or the influence of the laws of association on the imagination. Since the ideas of cause and effect are joined together only on the subjective basis of customary association, the inference has only subjective validity. Hume applied this conclusion rigorously to our inferences about external bodies and the personal self. Nevertheless, he was dissatisfied with his own atomistic view of the self as a congeries of perceptions, since his experience seemed to imply a knowledge of the substantial unity and causal power of the self, which his principles would not allow. He admitted a loose inference to the existence of a supreme intelligence but restricted religion to a purely speculative recognition of this intelligence, having no practical import. His theory of the passions extended mechanism into the affective order and assigned a subordinate role to reason. Hume sought associative ways of cultivating our other-regarding impulses, so that the social system itself might have a basis in the stable, customary laws of human nature.

BIBLIOGRAPHICAL NOTE

1. *Sources.* There is no collected critical edition of Hume's works. A collection of his philosophical writings was edited by T. H. Green and T. H. Grose: *The Philosophical Works of David Hume,* 4 Vols. (London: Longmans, Green, 1874–1875); this edition was reprinted in two series: Vol. I and II appeared as *A Treatise on Human Nature and Dialogues concerning Natural Religion,* 2 Vols. (New York: Longmans, Green, 1909), whereas Vol. III and IV were issued separately as *Essays Moral, Political and Literary,* 2 Vols. (New York: Longmans, Green, 1898). The Green-Grose edition is still interesting because of the editorial introductions and notes, written from the standpoint of idealism, which triumphed briefly

over empiricism in England during the latter part of the nineteenth century. Later scholars have preferred to refer to the two following editions prepared by L. A. Selby-Bigge: *A Treatise of Human Nature* (Oxford: Clarendon, 1888), and *Enquiries concerning the Human Understanding and concerning the Principles of Morals,* second ed. (Oxford: Clarendon, 1902), since these editions are enhanced by analytic indexes. For Hume's own summary of the *Treatise,* see his *An Abstract of a Treatise of Human Nature, 1740* (Cambridge: the University Press, 1938), ed. by J. M. Keynes and P. Sraffa.

As far as the two *Inquiries* are concerned, they are now most accessible in the well edited editions of C. W. Hendel: *An Inquiry concerning Human Understanding* (Indianapolis: Bobbs-Merrill, 1955), which also includes Hume's autobiography, *My Own Life,* as well as his *An Abstract of a Treatise of Human Nature* and *An Inquiry concerning the Principles of Morals* (Indianapolis: Bobbs-Merrill, 1957). The H. D. Aiken ed. of *Hume's Moral and Political Philosophy* (New York: Hafner, 1948) contains an important introductory essay by the editor. There is a compact reprinting of Hume, *Essays Moral, Political and Literary* (New York: Oxford University Press, 1963). Hume's esthetic writings are collected in: *Of the Standard of Taste and Other Essays* (Indianapolis: Bobbs-Merrill, 1965), ed. by J. W. Lenz. Selections from his historical writings are gathered by R. Popkin and D. F. Norton, eds., *David Hume: Philosophical Historian* (Indianapolis: Bobbs-Merrill, 1965). There are three important tools for studying Hume's religious position: *Dialogues concerning Natural Religion,* second ed. (Indianapolis: Bobbs-Merrill, 1963), ed. by N. K. Smith, whose 125-page Introduction is a basic presentation of the biographical and doctrinal material; *The Natural History of Religion* (Stanford: Stanford University Press, 1957), with an acute analysis by the editor, H. E. Root; R. Wollheim, ed., *Hume on Religion* (Cleveland: World Publishing Co., Meridian Books, 1964), containing not only the *Natural History* and *Dialogues* but also other pertinent passages. There are two modern collections of Hume's correspondence: the J. Y. T. Greig ed. of *The Letters of David Hume,* 2 Vols. (Oxford: Clarendon, 1932), and the R. Klibansky and E. C. Mossner ed. of *New Letters of David Hume* (Oxford: Clarendon, 1954). His earliest notations in philosophy are presented by E. C. Mossner, "Hume's Early Memoranda, 1729–1740: The Complete Text," *Journal of the History of Ideas,* 9 (1948), 492–518.

2. *Studies.* The best biography is E. C. Mossner, *The Life of David Hume* (Austin: University of Texas Press, 1954); still useful is J. Y. T. Greig, *David Hume* (New York: Oxford University Press, 1931). On the interweaving of ironic character and skeptical critique, see J. V. Price, *The Ironic Hume* (Austin: University of Texas, 1966). J. A. Passmore, *Hume's Intentions* (Cambridge: the University Press, 1952), examines the several levels of critical and reconstructive activity present in Hume. The centrality of moral aims in the science of man is the main theme in N. K. Smith's *The Philosophy of David Hume* (New York: St. Martin's

Press, 1964). Careful introductions to Hume's philosophy are made by: D. G. MacNabb, *David Hume: His Theory of Knowledge and Morality* (London: Hutchinson, 1951); B. M. Laing, *David Hume* (London: Benn, 1932); J. Laird, *Hume's Philosophy of Human Nature* (London: Metheun, 1932); A. H. Basson, *David Hume* (Baltimore: Penguin Books, 1958). There are two foreign-language introductions of very high competence: A. L. Leroy, *David Hume* (Paris: Presses Universitaires, 1953), and R. Metz, *David Hume, Leben und Philosophie* (Stuttgart: Frommann, 1929). R. F. Anderson, *Hume's First Principles* (Lincoln: University of Nebraska Press, 1966), gives a basic analysis.

A more extended analytic approach is made by A. Flew, *Hume's Philosophy of Belief* (New York: Humanities Press, 1961), which is a detailed, argued commentary on the first *Inquiry*. F. Zabeeh's *Hume, Precursor of Modern Empiricism* (The Hague: Nijhoff, 1961) also stresses the analytic relevance of Hume's epistemology, whereas G. Deleuze's *Empirisme et subjectivité: Essai sur la nature humaine selon Hume* (Paris: Presses Universitaires, 1953), shows Hume's bearing on a philosophy of human subjectivity. There are detailed accounts of Hume's theory of knowledge in: R. W. Church, *Hume's Theory of the Understanding* (Ithaca: Cornell University Press, 1935); C. Maund, *Hume's Theory of Knowledge* (New York: Macmillan, 1937); H. H. Price, *Hume's Theory of the External World* (Oxford: Clarendon, 1940). The interplay of reason and passion in Humean moral philosophy is a debated issue between: R. M. Kydd, *Reason and Conduct in Hume's Treatise* (New York: Oxford University Press, 1946); A. B. Glathe, *Hume's Theory of the Passions and of Morals* (Berkeley: University of California Press, 1950); R. D. Broiles, *The Moral Philosophy of David Hume* (The Hague: Nijhoff, 1964). The moral and political position is examined by: J. B. Stewart, *The Moral and Political Philosophy of David Hume* (New York: Columbia University Press, 1963); L. L. Bongie, *David Hume, Prophet of the Counter-Revolution* (Oxford: Clarendon, 1965).

The esthetic aspect of Hume is studied in T. Brunius, *David Hume on Criticism* (Stockholm: Almqvist and Wiksell, 1952), and O. Brunet, *Philosophie et esthétique chez David Hume* (Paris: Nizet, 1965). On his theory of God and religion, see: C. W. Hendel, *Studies in the Philosophy of David Hume,* new ed. (Indianapolis: Bobbs-Merrill, 1963), relating this theory to his entire philosophy; R. H. Hurlbutt, *Hume, Newton, and the Design Argument* (Lincoln: University of Nebraska Press, 1965), on the Newtonian popularizers; A. L. Leroy, *La Critique et la religion chez David Hume* (Paris: Alcan, 1930). A medieval forerunner of Hume is portrayed by J. R. Weinberg: *Nicolaus of Autrecourt, A Study in 14th Century Thought* (Princeton: Princeton University Press, 1948). The more immediate cultural milieu of Hume is treated by M. S. Kuypers, *Studies in the Eighteenth-Century Background of Hume's Empiricism* (Minneapolis: University of Minnesota Press, 1930), and more comprehensively by Basil Willey, *The Eighteenth-Century Background.*

3. *British Moralists and Scottish Realists.* Hume is fitted into the broad

context of moral thought by Basil Willey, *The English Moralists* (New York: Norton, 1964). Source materials are furnished by L. A. Selby-Bigge, ed.: *British Moralists,* 1-Vol. reprint (Indianapolis: Bobbs-Merrill, 1964), and by the J. M. Robertson ed. of Anthony Shaftesbury's influential *Characteristics of Men, Manners, Opinions, Times,* 1-Vol. reprint (Indianapolis: Bobbs-Merrill, 1964). Studies of the moral sense school are made by: D. D. Raphael, *The Moral Sense* (Oxford: Clarendon, 1947); J. Bonar, *Moral Sense* (New York: Macmillan, 1930). Bishop Butler is the subject of three competent studies: E. C. Mossner, *Bishop Butler and the Age of Reason* (New York: Macmillan, 1936); W. J. Norton, *Bishop Butler: Moralist and Divine* (New Brunswick: Rutgers University Press, 1940); A. Duncan-Jones, *Butler's Moral Philosophy* (Baltimore: Penguin Books, 1952). On Hume's Scottish friend, Hutcheson, see W. R. Scott, *Francis Hutcheson* (Cambridge: the University Press, 1900). The Scottish school's achievements are examined by one of its last representatives, James McCosh, *The Scottish Philosophy* (London: Macmillan, 1875), as well as by S. A. Grave, *The Scottish Philosophy of Common Sense* (Oxford: Clarendon, 1960).

INDEX

Abstraction, 27 ff, 109; critique of, 60 ff
Analogy, 84 f, 102, 134 f
Analysis and synthesis, 33; see Elementarism
Association, 22, 25, 98 f, 108 f, 119 ff; passional and moral, 140 f
Atheism, 70
Attention, 15

Bacon, Francis, 6, 79 n
Bayle, Pierre, 69 f, 88, 96, 99
Being, 22, 72 f, 92; see Existence
Belief, 4, 8, 40, 42, 109 f, 123 f
Bentham, Jeremy, 143
Berkeley, compared with Hume, 70 n, 74, 76 f, 80 f, 84, 90; compared with Locke, 57, 59, 60 ff, 65 ff, 70 f, 73 f, 79 f, 82, 87, 91; critique of abstraction, 60 ff; definition and reality of sensible things, 65 ff, 75 ff; God's reality and function, 77 f, 83 ff; mathematics and natural philosophy, 87 ff; nature, 89; New Principle, 60 ff; notion-relation-will, 81 ff; other finite minds, 85 ff; rejection of matter, 69 ff; theory of minds, 79 ff
Biran, Maine de, 119 n
Boyle, Robert, 1, 4, 37
Butler, Joseph, 134 n, 137

Cajetan, 84
Cambridge Platonists, 3, 8, 9 n, 10, 12, 32, 44
Causality, and association, 108 ff, 114 f; critique of, 115 ff, 131; and matter, 73; and nature, 89 f; uncritical account of, 22 ff, 39 f
Certitude, 8, 36, 112 ff
City of God, 92
Clarke, Samuel, 57, 116, 133 f, 136 f, 142
Coleridge, S. T., 59
Common good, 51 f
Common sense, 3, 103; and sensible things, 65 f, 74 f; and skepticism, 98
Consciousness, 26 f, 81, 129 f; see Experience, Perception, Reflection, Self

Considering act, 63
Cudworth, Ralph, 3
Custom, 22, 89 f, 119 f; and prediction, 132 f

Deism, 42, 135
Demonstration, 8, 35 ff, 39, 83 ff, 112 ff, 117, 123 f, 133 ff
Descartes and Cartesian factor, 1, 7, 22, 32, 44, 57, 59, 61, 70 n, 73, 82; attention, 15; demonstrative ideal, 8, 33, 35 ff, 38, 112, 114, 121 ff; elementarism, 6; ideas as formal and objective, 29; and immaterialism, 12; and qualities, 20, 104; and self, 26 f, 38 f, 81; see Rationalist strain in empiricism
Determinism, 45, 131 ff
Dewey, John, 13, 122 n
Dionysius the Pseudo-Areopagite, 84
Divine right of kings, 45
Doubt, 35, 99

Edwards, Jonathan, 92
Egocentric predicament, 68
Elementarism, 6, 33, 102; logical basis, 106 f
Empiricism, 3 ff, 13, 32 f, 42, 121 ff, 141 f; and causality, 117; criterion, 104 f; immaterialist, 60; prospective and retrospective, 128 n; and skepticism, 99
Epistemology, 4, 7
Essence, 22, 28 ff; nominal and real, 31 ff
Ethics; see Moral philosophy
Events, 106 n
Existence, atomistic principle of, 114, 130 f; and coexistence, 34 f, 37 f, 113; double, 126 f; and existential judgment, 36; and imagination, 107 f; individual, 30 f; internal and perishing, 127; knowledge of real, 38 ff, 83 ff, 126 ff; persons and things, 92; two kinds, 60 ff, 69, 73; world and self, 126 ff
Experience, 13, 60, 113, 117, 121 f; see Empiricism
External world, 76 f, 126 ff

149